Learning
SCIENCE
and the Science of
LEARNING

SCIENCE EDUCATORS' ESSAY COLLECTION

Learning SCIENCE and the Science of LEARNING

Edited by Rodger W. Bybee

NSTApress®

NATIONAL SCIENCE TEACHERS ASSOCIATION
Arlington, Virginia

NATIONAL SCIENCE TEACHERS ASSOCIATION

Claire Reinburg, Director
Judy Cusick, Associate Editor
Carol Duval, Associate Editor
Betty Smith, Associate Editor

ART AND DESIGN Linda Olliver, Director
NSTA WEB Tim Weber, Webmaster
PERIODICALS PUBLISHING Shelley Carey, Director
PRINTING AND PRODUCTION Catherine Lorrain-Hale, Director
    Nguyet Tran, Assistant Production Manager
    Jack Parker, Desktop Publishing Specialist
PUBLICATIONS OPERATIONS Erin Miller, Manager
sciLINKS Tyson Brown, Manager

NATIONAL SCIENCE TEACHERS ASSOCIATION
Gerald F. Wheeler, Executive Director
David Beacom, Publisher

Learning Science and the Science of Learning
    NSTA Stock Number: PB158X
    ISBN: 0-87355-208-3
    Library of Congress Control Number: 2002101367
    Printed in the USA by Kirby Lithographic Company, Inc.
    Printed on recycled paper

Contents

Part 1

How Do Students Learn Science?

After a brief overview of the role of theory in science and in education, the author looks at the relationship between some historical learning theories and the teaching practices that flow from them. For example, how is the Socratic method consistent with what Socrates proposed about how people learn? What is behaviorist about behavioral objectives? Why is group work in line with constructivist learning theories? Science teachers are encouraged to examine their own theory-practice links.

Cognitive scientists have studied the highly organized and efficiently utilized characteristics of experts' knowledge in thinking and problem solving. The authors discuss the important implications of this body of research for how instruction should be structured for prospective teachers and other students. They conclude by discussing a series of desirable attributes for science courses that derive from the science of learning research.

Part 2

Designing Curriculum for Student Learning

What we know about student learning establishes links between scientific inquiry and the science curriculum. In this chapter, the author discusses scientific inquiry and current learning research. He then proposes that the science curriculum should be based on core concepts or "big ideas" from science domains; here the National Science Education Standards serve as a guide. Effective science instruction should parallel science inquiry and the processes of learning; here the BSCS 5E model supplies an example. The author supports teaching science as inquiry and provides science teachers with practical examples.

Language arts and science are perceived as competing for classroom time and attention, and science is often neglected. However, effective literacy instruction need not be at the expense of meaningful science instruction. The authors explore the potentially powerful linkages between science and literacy and suggest concrete ways that elementary teachers and middle and high school science teachers can simultaneously enhance science and language learning.

The authors discuss curriculum, instruction, and assessment and how their integration enables students to achieve a strong knowledge base in science. After examining conventional beliefs and more contemporary views of curriculum, instruction, and assessment, the authors demonstrate how various overlaps of any two of the three components affect science learning and literacy. The overlap of all three components leads to what the authors call the Zone of Optimal Learning.

Part 3

Teaching That Enhances Student Learning

A series of classroom vignettes and student conversations provides a glimpse into how our theoretical understanding of human learning translates into science classroom practice. The surprisingly large number of components operating in an effective classroom must interrelate with each other if students are to retain and use their science conceptual understandings. The author brings together ideas from neurobiology, learning theory, and developmental psychology and correlates them with the complex matrix of everyday classroom practice that allows students to gain science reasoning skills, conceptual understandings, and insight into the nature of the scientific enterprise.

Learner-centered science teaching begins with the stories of learners. Knowing our students, and thereby crafting lessons that account for their interests, experiences, and ambitions, can make science teaching vastly more effective. Whether studying molecules, momentum, or membranes, each student brings a unique perspective with variable interest. Learner-centered teachers use student perspectives as a launching point and maximize interest by giving students a voice in determining the direction of the science class.

Typical hands-on, cookbook laboratory experiences do an extremely poor job of making apparent and playing off students' prior ideas, engendering deep reflection, and promoting understanding of complex content. This chapter addresses how to transform traditional laboratory activities into experiences that are more congruent with how people learn, the National Science Education Standards, *and the nature of science.*

Part 4

Assessing Student Learning

Assessment in the classroom is more than tests and quizzes on Friday. It is an everyday feature of classroom life. Students and teachers use assessment, for example, when they gauge the quality of a response to a question, judge the accuracy of a diagram, or evaluate an oral report. Ensuing class discussions help students understand how their own efforts can be improved. Research indicates that such classroom practices, often called formative *assessment, are among the most powerful methods of improving learning.*

Assessment involves an ongoing investigation of student learning that influences teachers' planning and instruction. Multiple assessment strategies should be used to provide feedback to students and teachers. Such strategies include questioning, concept maps, reflective journals, written tests, observations, drawings, performance, and interviews. Assessment practices should be inclusive of all students as well as congruent with learning goals and instructional strategies.

Part 5

Professional Development and the Science of Learning

The authors consider the important relationship between standards-based curriculum implementation and professional development. They begin by looking at the key recommendations about student learning and then discuss how curriculum materials can embody these recommendations. Because the result is nontraditional curriculum materials, they then consider the role of professional development for increasing the effectiveness of those materials. Finally, they discuss a professional development strategy that begins with selecting materials for curriculum reform.

Groundbreaking research on learning and cognition has produced many new insights into how people learn. These findings conclusively dispel the idea that short-term and isolated learning experiences can produce powerful learning. This is especially true for teacher learning, given the complexity of teaching and the multifaceted role expert teachers must play. Teacher learning programs must become more collegial, in-depth, and longer in duration and must be tailored to the experience levels of the learners, be they novice or expert teachers.

Preface

Science teachers today face numerous initiatives, ranging from "No Child Left Behind" at the national level to assessments for each student in local classrooms. Teachers of science have the daunting task of translating these varied, and sometimes contradictory, efforts to improve science education into actions they can apply. I have found it interesting that all the initiatives have student learning as an ultimate aim. Granted, the clarity of this goal varies considerably, but regardless of the proposed solution to a perceived problem, the recommendations assume that students will learn more science. Professional developers assume their work will help science teachers enhance student learning. Publishers claim their science textbooks will increase learning. Ironically, even some agencies responsible for assessments assume the tests will result in greater learning!

Many concerns expressed by teachers also center on the challenges of helping their students learn science. Challenges can arise for a variety of reasons—when teachers hold the highest ideals of learning, believing that all students should understand the basic concepts of physics (or chemistry, biology, or Earth sciences); when they have misperceptions, such as thinking that inquiry-based instruction takes too much time away from learning essential content; and when they are faced with practical considerations, such as the need for students to do well on state or local assessments. In light of these challenges, it is in the interest of all teachers of science to understand and apply the basic principles of learning in their classroom practices.

The chapters in this yearbook explicitly use as their centerpiece a National Research Council (NRC) report, *How People Learn: Brain, Mind, Experience, and School* (Bransford, Brown, and Cocking, eds. 1999. Washington, DC: National Academy Press). The NRC report represents over four years of work and a landmark synthesis of research on human learning. To state the obvious, *How People Learn* has significant implications for how our society educates; for the design of curricula, instruction, assessment, and professional development; and, ultimately, for individual science teachers. Here, I will not review findings from the NRC report. Individual authors of the yearbook chapters do that in the context of the themes they address.

After an introduction by Harold Pratt, NSTA president 2001–2002, the yearbook chapters are grouped according to the following themes: How Do Students Learn Science?; Designing Curriculum for Student Learning; Teaching That

Enhances Student Learning; Assessing Student Learning; and Professional Development and the Science of Learning. The design of the yearbook and discussions by the authors are intended to bring the theme—Learning Science and the Science of Learning—as close as possible to you, the individual science teacher. I believe we have done the best we can to meet this objective.

Rodger W. Bybee
Editor

Acknowledgments

For many years, I have proposed that the National Science Teachers Association (NSTA) should have a yearbook. Other professional organizations, such as the National Council of Teachers of Mathematics (NCTM), have a yearbook that addresses a critical issue for the profession. In 1983, 1984, and 1985 NSTA did have yearbooks, which were edited by Faith Brown and David Butts (1983), Rodger Bybee, Janet Carlson, and Alan McCormack (1984), and Rodger Bybee (1985). The idea did not become part of NSTA. Now, we have a new opportunity. I gratefully acknowledge the leadership of Harold Pratt, NSTA president 2001–2002, for embracing the idea of a yearbook for NSTA and Gerry Wheeler, executive director of NSTA, David Beacom, NSTA publisher, and the NSTA Board for supporting the initiative.

After identification of the yearbook theme by Harold Pratt, I had advice and support from a small and dedicated advisory board. The advisory board for this yearbook consisted of the following individuals:

◆ Rodney Cocking,

◆ Angelo Collins,

◆ Joe Flynn, and

◆ Harold Pratt

The authors of this yearbook deserve acknowledgment. Without exception, they addressed the theme, prepared chapters with science teachers in mind, submitted manuscripts on time, and responded to reviewer recommendations. I have never worked with individuals of more dedication.

All manuscripts underwent review and subsequent revision. Reviewers completed their task in a thorough and timely manner. The following individuals completed reviews for this yearbook.

James Barufaldi, University of Texas at Austin
Hedi Baxter, BSCS, Colorado Springs, Colorado
Susan M. Blunck, University of Maryland–Baltimore County
Donald P. French, Oklahoma State University

April Gardner, BSCS, Colorado Springs, Colorado
Sherry Herron, BSCS, Colorado Springs, Colorado
Barbara Klemm, University of Hawaii
Nancy Landes, BSCS, Colorado Springs, Colorado
Mary Lightbody, Westerville City Schools, Westerville, Ohio
John Penick, North Carolina State University
Aimee Stephenson, BSCS, Colorado Springs, Colorado
Joseph Taylor, BSCS, Colorado Springs, Colorado
Pamela Van Scotter, BSCS, Colorado Springs, Colorado

Two NSTA staff contributed to this effort. Shirley Watt Ireton helped with the initial organization of the work and with the identification of several reviewers. Judy Cusick provided invaluable assistance with final editing and preparation of the yearbook for production.

Finally, I express my deepest appreciation to my executive assistant, Dee Miller, who supported the work and did a remarkable job of keeping track of authors, revisions of manuscripts, and hundreds of important details.

Rodger W. Bybee
Editor

National Science Teachers Association

Introduction

"Learning Science and the Science of Learning," the title of this yearbook and my theme as NSTA president, was chosen with the assumption that virtually every science teacher is a learner and wants to improve his or her practice. Most teachers believe that their personal learning is never finished. This book is dedicated to you, the professional science teacher, who makes a career of learning—your own and that of your students.

The yearbook was inspired by the recent seminal publication, *How People Learn; Brain, Mind, Experience, and School,* published by the National Research Council's National Academy Press (1999). This book was produced by a committee of scholars and practitioners under the leadership of John Bransford, Vanderbilt University. Although written by researchers about the results of research, *How People Learn* is a very readable, practical, and useful guide for practitioners that explains in everyday language how people of all ages learn. There are specific sections on learning science, mathematics, and history. The book not only addresses how students learn, but has chapters devoted to how teachers learn their content and how to teach it.

Three overarching research findings provide a framework of what educators know about learners and learning and about teachers and teaching. Although the language of these findings speaks of students, they come from our knowledge of how people of all ages and professions learn. I think it will be instructive to view these three findings from the perspective of science teachers continuing to learn their content and their practice of teaching.

Students come to the classroom with preconceptions about how the world works. If their initial understanding is not engaged, they may fail to grasp the new concepts and information that are taught, or they may learn them for purposes of a test but revert to their preconceptions outside of the classroom. (How People Learn, p.14)

As science teachers and science educators, we approach teaching, curriculum development, and assessment with our current conceptions about how the world of the classroom works, namely, how teachers should teach and how students learn. Our job as professionals is to find ways to take our current conceptions about learning and place them against new research, concepts, and information about learning as a way of examining and improving our practice. Our roles as professionals include internalizing new views of teaching and learning and therefore teaching in new effective ways and not simply engaging in new language.

To develop competence in an area of inquiry, students must: (a) have a deep foundation of factual knowledge, (b) understand facts and ideas in the context of the conceptual framework, and (c) organize knowledge in ways that facilitate retrieval and application. (How People Learn, p.16)

This finding can be applied to our knowledge of science and of pedagogy. Outstanding teaching requires teachers to have a deep understanding of the subject matter and its structure, as well as an equally thorough understanding of the kinds of teaching activities that help students understand the subject matter in order to be capable of asking probing questions (*How People Learn*, p.188). Learning science means more than a superficial set of facts or explanations in most textbooks. It means understanding what we teach beyond what the textbooks provide us as content. It means being able to evaluate both the content and the learning activities suggested for the students. The interplay between content knowledge and understanding of pedagogy challenges the misconception about teaching that claims effective teaching means knowing the content and a generic set of teaching strategies that can be applied almost universally.

Too often the "facts" of our pedagogy are the tried and true methods we have used for years but are not grounded in a deep conceptual framework of the research on learning. The authors in this volume offer us an opportunity to reshape our deep foundation of pedagogical strategies in the research of learning rather than depending solely on our past practice.

In addition to inviting us to examine our own knowledge and practice, the authors offer us a context and framework through which we can examine our curriculum and the policies of our district and state that affect our teaching lives. Knowing the science of learning empowers teachers with the resources to argue for and support the decisions for curriculum and assessments that control much of their professional lives and the success of their students.

A metacognitive approach to instruction can help students learn to take control of their own learning by defining learning goals and monitoring their progress in achieving them. (How People Learn, p. 18)

Just as we should allow students the opportunity to verbalize and reflect on their own thinking, we as professionals must do the same. We must demand the time and support to set our own professional development goals and the opportunity to meet and discuss, plan, and review our teaching practices with the research on learning in mind.

With these three findings in mind, the content of the yearbook is useful and appropriate to a number of audiences.

◆ Schools and school districts will find the content useful as they consider what constitutes professional development and how organizational policies must change to support professional development programs.

◆ Professional developers will find the content useful as they design professional development opportunities.

◆ Science teachers will find the yearbook useful as they become more insightful consumers of professional development. They will become competent and discriminating in their selection and use of curriculum, instructional materials, teaching strategies, and assessments.

◆ Science educators in all roles will find the content useful as they become more effective proponents of enlightened policy and legislation that affect them and their students.

◆ Funding agencies and policymakers will find the yearbook useful as they decide what projects are worthwhile investments.

This yearbook is the result of the collaboration and contributions of the editor, authors, and the NSTA staff. My deep gratitude goes to Rodger Bybee, who suggested that yearbooks be reinstituted at NSTA and willingly agreed to edit and contribute to this volume. His leadership and contribution to this work, to the science education community throughout his career, and to me personally for many years is deeply appreciated. My thanks to Gerry Wheeler, NSTA's executive director, and David Beacom, NSTA's publisher, for enthusiastically accepting and supporting the idea of the yearbook. I thank the authors who willingly and capably accepted the assignment to write to my theme as president in such profound ways.

Harold Pratt
NSTA President 2001–2002

PART 1

How Do Students Learn Science?

How Students Learn and How Teachers Teach

Angelo Collins

Angelo Collins is the executive director of the Knowles Science Teaching Foundation. Her prior experiences include serving as the director of the *National Science Education Standards* project and the director of the INTASC Science Project and the Teacher Assessment Project. She also taught high school science for fifteen years. Her honors include the Outstanding Biology Teacher Award from the National Association of Biology Teachers and the Distinguished Alumni Award from the College of Education of the University of Wisconsin-Madison.

Not too long ago I asked a group of seventy-five middle grades science teachers how their students learn science. Many responded by stating the importance of motivation—"You've got to get them interested." Others responded by quoting from learning theories studied in university courses. Some mentioned Piaget's stages of learning, others referred to multiple intelligences, and still others spoke of learning styles. A few admitted that they were so concerned with their teaching, with the curriculum, with student behavior, and with state tests they simply hadn't thought about how students learn. I challenged these teachers to videotape some of their own teaching and see if they could identify any patterns that influenced their teaching decisions and practices. With the videotapes, they became increasingly aware of the relationship between their teaching and their ideas about how students learn. Only after several months did we personalize their patterns with a title—for example, Janice's Learning Theory.

In this chapter I explore relationships between learning theories and teaching practices. I compare three features of scientific and educational theories, provide a brief overview of some historically noteworthy learning theories and the teaching practices they inform, review contemporary learning theories, and conclude with implications for teaching practice.

A Comparison of Three Features of Theories

The *National Science Education Standards* (NRC 1996) maintains that understanding an idea implies a rich cluster of facts, concepts, and examples associated with the major idea. With the hope of increasing understanding, in this section I reflect on three ideas that have an impact on a science teacher's use of the term *theory*. First I look at a definition and the role of theories in science and in teaching. I then compare students' misconceptions in science and teachers' misconceptions in teaching. Finally I examine the place of theories in the work of professionals and technicians.

Definition and Role of Theory

As science teachers, with the emphasis on the *science* part, we are quite familiar with theories. The atomic theory, the theory of evolution by natural selection, the theory of gravity, and the theory of plate tectonics are just a few examples of familiar scientific theories. We know, even if the knowledge has become tacit, that a theory is a set of principles (laws) that together help us describe, explain, and predict natural events and phenomena. We recognize that two measures of the power of a theory are the number and the variety of events and phenomena it can explain and predict. We recall that the simpler a theory is, the more useful it is. We accept that theories change. For example, we no longer accept the theory that the Earth is the center of the universe, as this theory is no longer useful in explaining celestial phenomena. As science teachers, we readily acknowledge that theories are essential to the practice of science.

However, as science teachers, with the emphasis on the *teacher* part, we tend to disdain, distrust, or disregard educational theories. Somehow we have created a chasm between educational theory and teaching practice. We assume that educational theory informs and is informed by research conducted at places very far from our own classrooms with students very different from the ones we teach. Consequently, these educational theories seem to have little relevance for our own teaching practice.

Nevertheless, educational theories of learning are as essential to the practice of teaching as science theories are to the practice of science. Theories of learning provide a set of principles (laws) that help us describe, explain, and predict events and phenomena of learning such as understanding, remembering, forgetting, and creating. Theories of learning inform our practice of teaching. The same two measures of power—the number and the variety of events and phenomena explained and predicted—are equally true of learning theories as they are of science theories. As with scientific theories, theories of learning also change.

Personal Theories and Misconceptions

As science teachers, we expect that our students come to class with ideas they have learned in other courses as well as with naive, incomplete, inaccurate, inconsistent, non-canonical theories that they have invented to help them make sense of their experiences of the natural world. We call these personal theories "misconceptions," although they might be concepts, principles, or theories. Often these personal theories are not well-articulated although they are firmly held. We know the students' personal theories are firmly held in part because they have been so successful in helping the students make sense of the world.

We come to teach a science class with ideas of how students learn that we have acquired from courses, workshops, and professional reading. We must acknowledge, however, that we may hold naive, incomplete, inaccurate, non-canonical, and unexamined theories that we have invented to help us make sense of the successes and failures of our students. These personal theories also may be firmly held, although not well-articulated.

Professionals and Technicians

As science teachers, we generally agree that both scientists and technicians support the scientific enterprise. Scientists are expected to understand the theory and know the techniques practiced in the laboratory and field. Technicians are expected to make the techniques work smoothly and efficiently.

Once upon a time, fifty years ago, teachers were considered technicians. They employed instructional techniques, but the supporting theories of learning and teaching were dictated by the school administrator. Today, science teachers recognize that teaching is a profession requiring both practical and theoretical knowledge. It is practical in that we use our knowledge and skill to teach some *thing* to some *one* at some *time*—for example, we teach photosynthesis to Deborah on Tuesday at 10 a.m. But these teaching practices are informed by a set of principles, which, when concerned with how students learn, constitute a learning theory. Using both practical and theoretical knowledge, teachers are expected to engage in a teaching practice that both is elegant and enables all students to attain understanding and ability.

Examples of Historically Significant Learning Theories

For a long time philosophers and psychologists have struggled with ideas associated with learning. For example, what do terms such as *idea*, *concept*, *image*, *thinking*, *learning*, *knowing*, *understanding*, *remembering*, *forgetting*, and *creativity* mean? In the next section I comment on a few philosophers and psychologists whose learning theories have had an impact on teaching practice.

Philosophers

The first recorded efforts in Western civilization to describe what it means to know and to learn are captured in the *Meno,* written by the philosopher Plato in 400 B.C.E. (1981). In this dialogue, Plato attempts to capture the beliefs and practices of his teacher, Socrates. One of the ways Socrates taught was by using stories. Stories allowed his students to see familiar items, events, and phenomena in new ways. These stories were followed by what today we might call divergent and probing questions. From the stories and questions, students began to develop knowledge by relying on what they already knew—their prior knowledge. Plato, however, puzzled about the *origins* of both the initial and new knowledge. He provides his thoughts on the origin of human knowledge in *The Republic* (400 B.C.E.) (1955). Here, Plato tells the myth of the soldier, Er. Er appeared to be slain in battle but then appeared two weeks later in the realm of the everlasting and reported on his experiences. In this realm, souls waited to choose a new life. But prior to entering the new life, each soul had to drink from the River of Forgetfulness. Some drank more than others. Those who drank a lot would find it very difficult to learn in their new lives. For Plato, knowledge was innate; each person was born with knowledge. Experiences and observations in the realm of the everlasting determined the amount and type of that knowledge. How easily one learned and remembered depended on how much one had drunk from the River of Forgetfulness. For Plato, teaching meant helping a student become aware of what is already known. He constructed a theory that would explain what he had observed and experienced as a teacher, student, and philosopher. His teaching practice of telling stories and asking questions was invented to enable students to recall what they already knew. For Plato, learning theory and teaching practice informed one another.

While Plato and Socrates and Er and the River of Forgetfulness may seem quite distant, the questions Plato attempted to answer—why different students learn different things from the same lesson, why some students learn more than others, why some students do not seem to be able to remember—plague teachers today. And the contemporary pedagogical technique called the Socratic method has one of its roots in the learning theory that knowledge is innate and is called forth by questioning.

Another ancient philosopher who offered theories on how people learn was Aristotle. He believed that all mental life could be explained in terms of two basic components: elements (ideas) and the associations (links) between them. He proposed three associated laws of learning and memory, which today we might call a learning theory: (1) the Doctrine of Association by Contiguity, which stated that events or objects that occur in the same time or space are associated in memory, (2) the Doctrine of Association by Similarity, which stated that events or objects that are in any way similar are associated in memory, and (3) the Doctrine of Association by Contrast, which stated that events or objects that are opposite tend to be associated in memory.

In the seventeenth century, the philosopher John Locke accepted the Aristotelian idea that knowledge consists of linked ideas. However, he puzzled, as had Plato, over the origin of initial knowledge. Locke did not accept that there was a River of Forgetfulness and did not find Plato's theory very powerful. Locke proposed that all knowledge comes from experience and experience comes through the senses. He further proposed that a child is born as a blank slate *(tabula rasa)* with certain internal, "wired" capacities to link experiences to form ideas. Simple ideas necessarily precede complex ones.

Last spring I listened as a student teacher responded to a whiney student query— "Do we *have* to take notes?"— by saying, "Yes, hearing and writing helps you remember." Her personal learning theory, that the senses are the beginning of learning, was aligned with Locke's. It had an intuitive appeal and provided her with a reason for her instructional practice. The role of the senses in learning is dominant in many learning theories.

Psychologists

Wilhelm Wundt is frequently identified as the father of psychology. In 1879 he opened a laboratory to generate experimental data to study the human mind and behavior. One of the assumptions of this early psychologist was that all observations had to be made independent of the observer. John B. Watson reinforced this assumption in

1913 in his piece "Psychology as Behaviorists View It," published in the *Psychological Review*. Watson stated that there was no reliable way to validate by introspection what was going on in one's own mind. Only externally observable behaviors could be studied reliably and validly. Neither Wundt nor Watson would value the reflective practices used to promote learning that are so predominant today.

E. L. Thorndike was a prominent psychologist of the same period. He accepted the strongly held beliefs of his time—that humans are "hard-wired" to link experiences, that experiences are the source of ideas, and that only observable acts (behaviors) can be studied. Thorndike did his research on cats and how they learned to escape from a locked box. From this research, he proposed a human learning theory that had two principles. The first principle is the law of exercise, according to which the more a behavior is practiced or exercised, the more strongly it is established or learned. The second principle is the law of effect. According to this principle, if the response to a stimulus has a pleasing effect, then the probability of the learner repeating the response given the same stimulus increases. Similarly, if the response had an unpleasant effect, the less likely the same stimulus would elicit a similar response.

These early theories of behaviorism provide the foundation for the well-recognized instructional technique of drill and practice. This theory supports the belief that if solving one problem at the end of the chapter is a good thing, doing all of them is even better. The idea of giving rewards for showing the desired behavior underlies the practice of some teachers who hold out the promise of no homework on the weekend if all the weekly assignments are completed accurately and on time.

Beginning in the late 1930s, working with rats and pigeons in a laboratory and applying the learning of these animals to human learning, B. F. Skinner (1966) made great advances in refining behaviorism as learning theory. For example, he found that rewards do not need to accompany every desired stimulus-response reaction. Rewards could be given randomly and infrequently. He also found that he could shape behaviors. He would break a large task into smaller subtasks. Then he would reward the appropriate stimulus-response behaviors of the subtasks. The subtasks would accumulate sequentially until the target task became a habit. Tasks requiring simple behaviors could be chained for more complex tasks.

Surely a major legacy of the theory of learning developed by B. F. Skinner is the prominence of and reliance on behavioral objectives in designing instruction. Behavioral objectives, which are more limited than widely used instructional objectives (goals for learning), are always written in terms of how many students will achieve the desired response at what level of success in what amount of time. The response is always written in terms of observable behaviors. Certain verbs, such as *describe*, *compare*, and *label*, are useful in writing behavioral objectives. Other verbs, such as *appreciate*, which do not describe behaviors, may not be used. The classic text for learning to write behavioral objectives is *Preparing Objectives for Programmed Instruction* (Mager 1962).

Behaviorism as a learning theory has many attractive features: It is simple, it can be used to explain many phenomena associated with learning, and it is based on controlled research. However, behaviorism is also based on the assumption that learning theorists cannot know what is going on in the mind. Although behaviorists claim to be scientific, the fact that they use only what is observable to explain and predict learning is a rather narrow definition of being scientific. For example, we as scientists do not observe gravity; we only observe the effects of gravity. However, gravity is not disallowed from science because it is not observable.

Another fundamental question about behaviorism is whether we are willing to equate and limit all learning to observable behaviors. Behaviorism is a good theory for explaining behaviors, and there are certain school activities that we as science teachers want students to engage in "without thinking." For example, when students take out Bunsen burners they automatically put on safety goggles without constructing a meaning for fire, danger, and safety. But today phenomena such as knowing, understanding, and being creative are considered more than behaviors.

All of the learning theories described so far are considered "passive" learning theories. In each, the student is the recipient of knowledge from an external source. Each theory was developed to explain and predict learning phenomena and was useful for a time, but eventually these theories waned in significance as an increasing number of phenomena were identified that the theories could not explain.

Contemporary Learning Theories

Contemporary learning theories are active and are frequently termed *cognitive* (in opposition to *behavioral*). They assume that learning requires activity on the part of the learner—that something is happening in the mind and that it is possible to infer what that is from the actions of the person engaged in learning. In this section I report on some forerunners of contemporary learning theories and on constructivism, the predominant learning theory today.

Early Cognitive Scientists

Many contemporary learning theories assume that the activity of attaining understanding is building knowledge structures—that is, relationships between and among ideas. John Dewey (1900), who held that for learning to take place students had to actively engage in meaningful problem solving, was among the first to propose an active learning theory. The Gestalt psychologists of the late nineteenth and early twentieth century, also active learning theorists, believed that ideas were received whole and fit together like pieces of a puzzle in a moment of insight.

Jean Piaget's learning theory (Piaget and Inhelder 1969; Piaget 1975) assumes that there are two ways to structure knowledge. One is assimilation—fitting new ideas into existing structures. The other is accommodation—reorganizing existing knowledge structure so that the new ideas fit. Piaget's theory that a learner has to work with concepts of concrete objects and events before structuring abstract concepts has an impact on today's teaching. When you begin science instruction with concrete objects and hands-on activities, Piaget has influenced your learning theory.

Information processing is another active learning theory. It posits that the activity of the human mind is like the activity of a computer. Information is received through the senses, "processed" in small bits in short-term memory, and stored in long-term memory. When you instruct students to diagram concept maps to represent what they know, information processing has influenced you.

As we get closer to current theories and practices, it becomes increasingly difficult to identify a theory with a single person. The theories have not been sufficiently tested by time for the identities of enduring persons to have emerged. However, Rumelhart (1977) and Norman (1982) wrote extensively on information processing. Nobel Laureate Herbert Simon (1996) is considered the father of artificial intelligence, an area closely associated with information processing. Novak and Gowin (1984) are well-known for their seminal work on concept maps.

Conceptual change is another active learning theory that has had a great impact on science teaching. Many investigators have contributed to the theory of conceptual change and the closely aligned study of misconceptions. According to conceptual change theory, students come to class with well-developed knowledge structures they have built to explain their natural worlds. Some of the ideas in their knowledge structures are naive and are termed *misconceptions*. Helping students realize the limits of their current conceptions is the first step in conceptual change. Discrepant events are intended to influence this realization. The effort by Rosalind Driver and her colleagues (1983, 1994) to identify students' misconceptions is one important effort to understand misconceptions.

Constructivism

Without a doubt, *constructivism* is the most frequently used term associated with human learning today. However, it is a term with multiple meanings. To philosophers, constructivism is an epistemological theory referring to the very nature of knowledge. Cognitive psychologists use the term to describe human learning. Those who design instructional materials and techniques use the term *constructivism* to refer to a set of design principles that inform teaching; some call these principles, and constructivism, a theory of teaching.

Despite the multiplicity of connotations, there are some recognized features of constructivism: learning is active; learning is the interaction of ideas and processes; new knowledge is built on prior knowledge; learning is enhanced when situated in contexts that students find familiar and meaningful; complex problems that have multiple solutions enhance learning; and learning is augmented when students engage in discussions of the ideas and processes involved.

This brief overview does not do justice to recent efforts by current cognitive scientists and others to describe, explain, and predict how people learn. For a more in-depth look at the subject, readers can examine the National Research Council's comprehensive report *How People Learn: Brain, Mind, Experience, and School* (Bransford, Brown, and Cocking 1999), which provides a readily understood synthesis of current learning theories. The authors of many chapters in *Learning Science and the Science of Learning* refer to that book and/or expand on facets of constructivism.

Conclusion

After watching videotapes of her classes, Janice, the teacher named in the introduction, realized that her instruction included many activities that students conducted in groups. She knew these activities kept students' interest, and it was her belief that a person needs to be interested and attentive in order to learn. Group work and presentations also supported her belief that you learn when you teach others.

Janice did find that some of her practices were not consistent with the personal learning theory she wanted to espouse, such as her insistence that all students write in black ink. And she found that some aspects of the personal learning theory she was developing did not yet influence her practice. For example, she intended to try having different groups of students do different but related activities to generate more opportunities for discussion and mutual teaching.

Science teachers who develop personal learning theories to inform their practice join with philosophers, psychologists, and most recently, sociologists and neurobiologists who continue to ask what it means to know, to understand, to inquire, or to create. These professionals continue to develop and refine powerful learning theories to explain and predict learning phenomena and to improve teaching practice.

References

Bransford, J. D., Brown, A. L., and Cocking, R. R., eds. 1999. *How people learn: Brain, mind, experience, and school.* Washington, DC: National Academy Press.

Dewey, J. 1900. *The school and society.* Chicago: University of Chicago Press

Driver, R. 1983. *The pupil as scientist?* Buckingham, UK: Open University Press, Milton Keynes

Driver, R., Squires, A., Rushworth, P., and Wood-Robinson, V. 1994. *Making sense of secondary science.* New York: Routledge.

Mager, R. F. 1962. *Preparing objectives for programmed instruction.* San Francisco: Fearon Publishers.

National Research Council (NRC). 1996. *National science education standards.* Washington, DC: National Academy Press.

Norman, D. A. 1982. *Learning and memory.* New York: W.H. Freeman.

Novak, J., and Gowin, D. B. 1984. *Learning how to learn.* Cambridge: Cambridge University Press.

Piaget, J. 1975 *The development of thought.* New York: Viking Press.

Piaget, J., and Inhelder, B. 1969. *The psychology of the child.* New York: Basic Books.

Plato. *Meno*, trans. Benjamin Jowett. 1981. Indianapolis: Bobbs-Merrill:

Plato. *The Republic*, trans. H. D. P. Lee. 1955. Hamondsworth, Middlesex: Penguin Books.

Rumelhart, D. E. 1977. *Introduction to human information processing.* New York: John Wiley.

Simon, H. A. 1996. *The sciences of the artificial*. Boston: MIT Press.

Skinner, B. F. 1966. *Science and human behavior.* New York: Macmillan.

Watson, J. B. 1948. Psychology as behaviorists view it. In W. Dennis, ed., *Readings in the history of psychology*, 47. New York: Appleton-Century-Crofts.

Applying the Science of Learning to the Education of Prospective Science Teachers

José P. Mestre and Rodney R. Cocking

José P. Mestre is a professor of physics at the University of Massachusetts Amherst. His professional interests include cognitive studies of problem solving in physics as well as applying research findings to the design of instructional strategies that promote active learning. He has served on boards and committees for the National Research Council, the National Science Foundation, the College Board, the Educational Testing Service, and the American Association of Physics Teachers. He has published numerous research and review articles on science teaching and learning, and has coauthored or coedited fifteen books.

Rodney R. Cocking is program director for Learning and Developmental Sciences and the Children's Research Initiative at the National Science Foundation. He is on leave from his position as senior program officer at the National Academy of Sciences, where he was founding director of the Board on Behavioral, Cognitive, and Sensory Sciences. His contributions to the field of cognition include the books *Blueprints for Thinking; Cognitive Development from Childhood to Adolescence; Structure and Development in Child Language;* and *How People Learn,* with John Bransford and Ann Brown, and the monograph *The Science of Learning,* with José Mestre. He is cofounder and editor of the *Journal of Applied Developmental Psychology.*

Effective teachers need "pedagogical content knowledge"—knowledge about how to teach in particular disciplines, which is different from knowledge of general teaching methods. Expert teachers know the structure of their disciplines and this provides them with cognitive roadmaps that guide the assignments they give students, the assessments they use to gauge student progress, and the questions they ask in the give and take of classroom life. (Bransford, Brown, and Cocking 1999, xviii)

Over the last two decades, cognitive research has made great strides in helping us understand the learning process. It should not be surprising that findings from research on learning point to the ingredients that should be present in effective instruction. Perhaps the best synthesis of research on learning is contained in a recent report from the National Research Council/National Academy of Sciences (NRC/ NAS), *How People Learn: Brain, Mind, Experience, and School* (Bransford, Brown, and Cocking 1999). This report goes beyond synthesis and provides examples of how learning research can be applied in teaching. In this chapter, we provide a brief review of research on learning and discuss its implications for the preparation of prospective science teachers.

Portions of this article previously appeared in Mestre, J. P. 2001. Implications of research on learning for the education of science and physics teachers. *Physics Education* 21 (1): 44–51.

Overview of Research Findings Pertinent to Teaching and Learning Science

The Nature of Expertise

Much of what is known about knowledge acquisition, storage in memory, and application to solving problems has come from studies of experts engaged in solving problems in their areas of expertise. Experts have extensive knowledge that is highly organized and used efficiently in solving problems, and so cognitive scientists have focused on characterizing the organization, acquisition, retrieval, and application of experts' knowledge (see Chapter 2 of Bransford, Brown, and Cocking 1999). The organization of experts' knowledge is hierarchical, with the top of the hierarchy containing the major principles and concepts of the domain; ancillary concepts, related facts, and equations occupy the middle to lower levels of the knowledge pyramid (Chi and Glaser 1981; Glaser 1992; Larkin 1979; Mestre 1994). Because of the highly organized nature of their knowledge, experts are able to access their knowledge quickly and efficiently. Further, procedures for applying the major principles and concepts are closely linked to the principles and are retrieved with relatively little cognitive effort when a major principle is accessed in memory. This facility allows experts to focus their cognitive efforts on analyzing and solving problems, rather than on searching for the appropriate "tools" in memory needed to solve the problems. By virtue of having an efficient organizational structure of knowledge, experts need to spend relatively little effort to learn even more about their areas of expertise since new knowledge is integrated into the existing knowledge structure with the appropriate links to make recall and retrieval relatively easy.

Experts also approach problem solving differently from novices (Chi, et al. 1981). For example, when asked to categorize problems (without solving them) according to similarity of solution, experts categorize according to the major principles that can be applied to solve the problems, whereas novices categorize according to the superficial attributes of the problems (e.g., according to the objects or terms that appear on the problem statement). When asked to state an approach they would use to solve specific problems, experts discuss the major principle they would apply, the justification for why the principle can be applied to the problem, and a procedure for applying the principle. The expert (the adept learner) employs a systematic search and exploration of the problem space. In contrast, novices jump immediately to generating a solution.

This research suggests that the tacit knowledge that experts use to solve problems should be made explicit during instruction, and that students should actually practice applying this knowledge (no longer tacit) while solving problems. If one believes that learners learn by constructing knowledge (see next section), however, this cannot be accomplished simply by telling students how major ideas apply to problems. Students need to engage in applying and thinking about how the big ideas are relevant for solving particular problems so that they become internalized as useful problem-solving tools.

Current View of Learning

The contemporary view of learning is that *individuals actively construct the knowledge they possess* (see, e.g., Mestre and Cocking 2000). Constructing knowledge is a lifelong, effortful process requiring significant mental engagement from the learner. In contrast to the view of learning whereby knowledge is "absorbed in ready-to-use form," the "constructing knowledge" view has two important implications for teaching. One implication is that the knowledge that individuals already possess affects their ability to learn new information. When new knowledge conflicts with resident knowledge, the new information will not make sense to the learner, and is often constructed (or accommodated) in ways that are not optimal for long-term recall or for application in problem-solving contexts (Anderson 1987; Schauble 1990; Resnick 1983; Glasersfeld 1989). For example, when children who believe the Earth is flat are told that it is round, they assimilate this concept to mean that it is round like a pancake, with people standing on top of the pancake (Vosniadou and Brewer 1992). When subsequently told that the Earth is round not like a pancake, but rather round like a ball, children envision a ball with a pancake on top, upon which people could stand (after all, children reason, people would fall off if standing on the side of a ball!). Thus, prior knowledge and sense-making are prominent in the constructivist view of learning.

The second implication is that instructional strategies that facilitate the construction of knowledge should be favored over those that do not. Sometimes this statement is interpreted to mean that we should abandon all lecturing and adopt instructional strategies where students are actively engaged in their learning. Although the latter goal is certainly desirable, the former is an overreaction. It is certainly true that, under the right conditions, lecturing can be a very effective method for helping students learn, but wholesale lecturing is not an effective means of getting the majority of students engaged in constructing knowledge during class time. Hence, instructional approaches where students are discussing science, doing science, teaching each other science, and offering problem-solution strategies for evaluation by peers will facilitate the construction of science knowledge.

The Relationship between Content Expertise and Teaching

Expertise in a discipline is a necessary, but not sufficient, condition for teaching a discipline. An effective instructor also has a wealth of "pedagogical content knowledge," which includes knowledge about the types of difficulties that students experience, typical paths that students must traverse to achieve understanding, and potential strategies for helping students overcome learning obstacles, all of which are discipline-dependent (Bransford, Brown, and Cocking 1999). Pedagogical content knowledge also differs from knowledge about general teaching methods, which are often taught within "methods" courses outside of the science discipline. In an isolated methods course in, say, physics, it is difficult to teach such things as the types of assignments that are best suited for teaching particular topics, the types of assessments that are best suited to gauge students' progress and to guide instruction, and the way to structure classroom discussions to highlight and clarify new ideas, as well as to integrate them within the students' knowledge structures. In short, there is an interaction between knowledge of the discipline and the pedagogy for teaching that discipline that results, for the experienced instructor, in a "cognitive road map" that guides the instructor while teaching.

Assessment in the Service of Learning

Assessment, as it is carried out in most university science courses, is intended to sum up what the students have learned for the purpose of assigning grades. This is *summative assessment*. It is erroneously assumed that summative assessments also represent students' competence. Largely missing from science classrooms, especially large lecture courses, is *formative assessment*, which is intended to provide feedback during learning exercises to both students and instructors, so that students have an opportunity to revise and improve the quality of their thinking and instructors can tailor instruction appropriately. Perhaps the biggest deterrent to using formative assessments in science classes is that instructors lack techniques for using continuous formative assessment in ways that are unobtrusive and that fit seamlessly with instruction. The age-old technique of asking a question to the class and asking for a show of hands has been tried by most teachers, but it does not work well since few students participate in the hand-raising because they prefer to remain anonymous when it comes to admitting that they might not know an answer. But to ignore students' current level of understanding during the course of instruction is perilous because research on learning indicates that all new learning depends on the learner's prior learning and current state of understanding.

In small classes it is not difficult to shape teaching so that two-way communication takes place between the instructor and the student. For example, one very effective method of teaching physics to small classes, perfected by Minstrell (1989), involves class discussions led by the teacher. Students offer their reasoning for the entire class to consider (as well as the instructor), with the class format taking somewhat the form of a debate among students and with the instructor serving as moderator of the discussion to lead it in certain directions by posing carefully crafted questions. In large enrollment classes, new classroom communication systems allow students to work collaboratively on conceptual or quantitative problems, entering answers electronically via calculator-type key pads and then seeing the entire class's responses graphed in histogram form for discussion (see Chapter 7, Bransford, Brown, and Cocking 1999). The histogram serves as a springboard for a class discussion in which students volunteer the reasoning that led to particular answers and the rest of the class evaluates the arguments. The instructor moderates the discussion, making sure that it leads to appropriate understanding.

Transferring Knowledge Flexibly across Different Contexts

Transfer, which refers to the ability to apply knowledge learned in one context to a new problem or situation, is difficult to achieve with traditional instruction (Bransford, Brown, and Cocking 1999). Transfer is an important goal for teachers to keep in mind since it is, in essence, what *makes learning last*. Science teachers often complain that students do not apply what they learn in math classes to their science classes. Research consistently confirms that transfer is not easy to accomplish.

The scientific research evidence suggests that five features of learning affect transfer and whether or not it will be facilitated by the learning situation (see Chapter 3, Bransford, Brown, and Cocking 1999): (1) The amount of learning clearly affects whether the knowledge is available for transfer, and this depends on (2) the time on task and (3) students' interest and motivation to learn the material. (4) The context in which the knowledge is learned is also pivotal in promoting transfer; if knowledge is learned solely in one context, it is unlikely that the new knowledge will be transferable to other contexts. This implies that as new knowledge is learned, students should be assisted in considering multiple contexts in which it applies and in linking the new knowledge to previously learned knowledge. (5) Finally, new learning involves transfer from previous learning, and previous learning can interfere with ability to transfer knowledge appropriately to new contexts (the science education research literature on "preconceptions" or "alternative conceptions" is an archetypal example).

Metacognition

Thinking about Thinking: Becoming a Reflective Learner

The ability to use knowledge in new contexts—*transfer*—can be improved without resorting to explicit prompting by teaching students to use metacognitive strategies that are based on research from the area of *metacognition* (see Chapter 2, Bransford, Brown, and Cocking 1999). Metacognitive strategies refer to techniques for helping learners become more aware of themselves as learners (their ability to monitor their understanding, for example). This self-awareness as a learner includes a variety of self-regulation behaviors that relate to learners' reflective thinking: the ability to plan, monitor success, and correct errors when appropriate and the ability to assess one's readiness for high-level performance in the area one is studying and working to understand. Reflecting about one's own learning is a major component of metacognition, and does not occur naturally in science classrooms (or in many learning contexts), due to lack of opportunity and time for reflective thought and the fact that instructors do not emphasize its importance. It is common to hear science students comment, "I am stuck on this problem," but when asked to be more specific about this condition of "stuckness," students are at a loss to describe what it is about the problem that has them perplexed, and often they just repeat that they are just stuck and can't proceed. Students don't seem to be aware of themselves as learners. If, however, during instruction, teachers take the time to suggest why and how students should reflect about their learning, there are fewer incidents of the "stuck" condition, since students learn to identify what they are missing that would allow them to proceed. The "time out to reflect" is in itself a model for student learning—in order to learn that thought processes need to be consolidated periodically and that, as learners, they occasionally need to take stock of how their work is progressing.

Thinking about Doing: Selecting from the Learned Repertoire

A second kind of metacognition is learning to reflect on the types of problem-solving strategies one has learned in the past. While the first type of metacognition, discussed in the previous paragraph, is focused on *oneself as a self-monitoring learner,* there is also a meta-level to understanding how to select problem-solving strategies. That is, thinking about strategies and how strategies are selected for problem solving relates to students' deeper understanding of the possibilities—it is thoughtful behavior geared toward selection and application. Kuhn (2000) has shown that understanding *why* a particular strategy is preferable to others plays a critical role in determining whether an available strategy will be used. Kuhn believes that such meta-level understanding plays a critical role in students' sustaining their own learning management and problem solving once the teacher and other supports (peers in groups) are no longer present. *What makes learning last* is the ability to monitor one's thinking, including selecting from the knowledge base of strategies one has learned in the past. Failure to transfer is the major limitation of many educational approaches because they do not focus on deep understanding and applying strategies or on how to develop such knowledge in students (Kuhn 2000).

Active-Reflective Learners

Promoting the habit of reflecting on one's own learning (and on one's own thought processes) is pivotal in science courses that deviate from the norm in pedagogy. Despite the research evidence to indicate that students learn best when actively engaged, the lecture format is the instructional model that most prospective science teachers experience in their college training, a format that encourages passive note-taking. Worse, note-taking is often seen by the teacher and student alike as "active engagement." Courses that attempt to get students to work collaboratively, or that try other techniques to engage them, are often viewed by students as gimmicks, and thus simply to be tolerated rather than invested in. In cases such as these, teachers need to communicate with students why the course is being taught the way it is, and explain how research on learning suggests that the approach being used is superior to teach-by-telling approaches. Only by getting students to become reflective learners, and by providing opportunities for them to accrue evidence that the "active learning" approaches help them learn more than the lecture approach, will they begin to achieve "buy-in" and become active participants in their own learning, rather than simply tolerant participants.

What Research Suggests about Courses
for Prospective Science Teachers

The science of learning research evidence carries important implications for how instruction should be structured for prospective teachers (and all students for that matter). Here we provide a list of desirable attributes for science courses suggested by that research. The list of attributes is not intended to be complete, and is very likely somewhat idiosyncratic; others' lists will likely differ, but if any two lists based on cognitive research findings are compared, there should be considerable overlap. Further, the list is intentionally general and does not differentiate between courses aimed at the elementary, middle, or high school levels. Finally, no hierarchy is implied by this list.

◆ **Science content and pedagogy should be integrated.**

When pedagogy and content are taught separately, they are seldom integrated. An ideal course for prospective teachers integrates the subject content with effective ways of teaching that content, the goal being to develop pedagogical content knowledge. Just as we have argued that what we know about students' learning comes from the science of learning, pedagogy needs to be grounded in scientific investigations as well, and subject content and pedagogy need to be presented together to teachers.

◆ **Construction and sense-making of science knowledge should be encouraged.**

Most college professors think that by telling students ideas clearly enough the students will learn the ideas. Although teachers can facilitate learning, the research evidence indicates that students must do the learning themselves. Students must also learn science content in ways that make sense to them, and their understanding of that science must be consistent with scientists' current models for how the physical and biological worlds work. Classroom environments in which students are actively engaged and the instructor plays the role of learning coach (e.g., inquiry learning, cooperative group learning, hands-on activities) are helpful in achieving this goal.

◆ **The teaching of content should be a central focus.**

Clearly, any science course for prospective teachers has to be based on specific science content, but at the same time it should not be so laden with content details that it becomes a race to cover as many topics as possible. The emphasis should be on in-depth understanding in a few major topics rather than the memorization of facts about many topics; the former has lasting value, the latter is quickly forgotten after the course is over. The former is more likely to transfer; the latter is rarely related to other learning contexts.

◆ **Ample opportunities should be available for learning "the processes of doing science."**

Doing science requires more than memorizing lots of content facts; it also requires knowledge about the processes involved in scientific investigation and knowledge of the processes of science. Students should, therefore, use apparatus, objects, equipment, and technologies to design experiments and test hypotheses, rather than perform "cookbook" labs. Enough guidance should be provided so that students make suitable progress, but exploration and discovery are important scientific processes as well. They should learn the language of science and be able to explain their experiments in the vocabularies of science.

◆ **Ample opportunities should be provided for students to apply their knowledge flexibly across multiple contexts.**

In the physical sciences, it is usually the case that a handful of concepts can be applied to solve problems across a wide range of contexts. The transfer research literature suggests that when people acquire knowledge in one context they can seldom apply this knowledge to situations in related contexts that look superficially different from the original context, but which are related by the major idea that could be applied to solve or analyze them. The implication is that students should learn to apply major concepts in multiple contexts in order to make the knowledge "fluid." Other sciences that have larger sets of concepts also require practice for students to relate the concepts to new and varied situations. To repeat what has been said before, providing practice exercises across a variety of contexts and situations is what makes learning last—it is the way to promote *transfer of learning*.

◆ **Helping students organize content knowledge according to some hierarchy should be a priority.**

To learn lots of details about a topic, to recall that knowledge efficiently, and to apply it flexibly across different contexts requires a highly organized mental framework. A hierarchical organization—in which the major principles and concepts are near the top of the hierarchy, and ancillary ideas, facts, and formulas occupy the lower levels of the hierarchy but are linked to related knowledge within the hierarchy—is needed if a learner is to achieve a high level of proficiency in a field. One technique that has been employed successfully to help students both discern the hierarchical structure of science knowledge and organize that knowledge into their mental frameworks is *concept mapping* (Novak 1998).

◆ **Qualitative reasoning based on concepts should be encouraged.**

Much of the knowledge that scientists possess is referred to as "tacit knowledge"; it is frequently used knowledge that is seldom made explicit or verbalized (e.g., when applying conservation of mechanical energy, one must make sure that there are no nonconservative forces doing work on the system). Working with principles tacitly is fine for experts, but tacit knowledge should be made explicit to novice learners so that they recognize it, learn it, and apply it. One way of making tacit knowledge explicit is by constructing qualitative arguments using the science that is being learned. By both constructing qualitative arguments and evaluating others' arguments, students can begin to appreciate the role of conceptual knowledge in "doing science."

◆ **Metacognitive strategies should be taught so that students learn how to learn.**
Students should learn to be able to predict not only their ability to perform tasks but also their current levels of mastery and understanding. Helping students to be self-reflective about their own learning will assist them in *learning how to learn* more efficiently. For example, when stuck trying to solve a problem, asking oneself questions such as, "What am I missing or what do I need to know to make progress here?"; "In what ways is this problem similar to others I've seen before?"; and "Am I stuck because of a lack of knowledge or because of an inability to identify or implement some procedure for applying a principle or concept?" are often helpful in deciding on a course of action. After solving a problem, reflecting on the solution by asking questions such as, "What did I learn that was new by solving this problem?"; "What were the major ideas that were applied and what is their order of importance?"; "Why did the instructor give this particular problem to us?"; and "Am I able to pose a problem in an entirely different context that can be solved with the same approach?" help one monitor mastery and understanding of the topics being learned. Teachers should implement these self-reflective strategies in problem-solving exercises by having students engage in post–problem-solving summaries that address these kinds of questions. In this way, students' own learning progress becomes more evident to them.

◆ **Formative assessment should be used frequently to monitor students' understanding and to help tailor instruction to meet students' needs.**
Formative assessment helps students realize what they don't understand (acting as an online monitoring of the learner's progress, so to speak), and formative assessment helps teachers craft tailored instructional strategies to help students achieve necessary and appropriate understanding in a particular learning exercise. The practice of using formative assessment strategies also models a very powerful pedagogical strategy that prospective teachers should adopt when they become teachers—that is, that learning needs to be monitored as it occurs, not as an after-the-fact product.

References

Anderson, C. W. 1987. Strategic teaching in science. In B. F. Jones, A. S. Palincsar, D. S. Ogle, and E. G. Carr, eds., *Strategic teaching and learning: Cognitive instruction in the content areas,* 73–91. Alexandria, VA: Association for Supervision and Curriculum Development.

Bransford, J. D., Brown, A. L., and Cocking, R. R., eds. 1999. *How people learn: Brain, mind, experience, and school.* Washington, DC: National Academy Press.

Chi, M. T. H., Feltovich, P. J., and Glaser, R. 1981. Categorization and representation of physics problems by experts and novices. *Cognitive Science* 5: 121–52.

Chi, M. T. H., and Glaser, R. 1981. The measurement of expertise: Analysis of the development of knowledge and skills as a basis for assessing achievement. In E. L. Baker and E. S. Quellmalz, eds., *Design, analysis and policy in testing,* 37–47. Beverly Hills, CA: Sage Publications.

Glaser, R. 1992. Expert knowledge and processes of thinking. In D. Halpern, ed., *Enhancing thinking skills in the sciences and mathematics,* 63–75. Hillsdale, NJ: Lawrence Erlbaum Associates.

Glasersfeld, E. 1989. Cognition, construction of knowledge, and teaching. *Synthese* 80: 121–40.

Kuhn, D. 2000. Why development does (and doesn't) occur: Evidence from the domain of inductive reasoning. In R. Siegler and J. McClelland, eds., *Mechanisms of cognitive development: Neural and behavioral perspectives.* Mahwah, NJ: Lawrence Erlbaum Associates.

Larkin, J. H. 1979. Information processing models in science instruction. In J. Lochhead and J. Clement, eds., *Cognitive process instruction,* 109–18. Hillsdale, NJ: Lawrence Erlbaum Associates.

Mestre, J. P. 1994. Cognitive aspects of learning and teaching science. In S. Fitzsimmons and L. C. Kerpelman, eds., *Teacher enhancement for elementary and secondary science and mathematics: Status, issues and problems,* 3-1–3-53.Washington, DC: National Science Foundation (NSF 94-80).

Mestre, J. P., and Cocking, R. R. 2000. The science of learning. Special Issue of *Journal of Applied Developmental Psychology* 21 (1): 1–135.

Minstrell, J. A. 1989. Teaching science for understanding. In L. B. Resnick and L. E. Klopfer, eds., *Toward the thinking curriculum: Current cognitive research,*129–49. Alexandria, VA: Association for Supervision and Curriculum Development.

Novak J. D. 1998. *Learning, creating, and using knowledge: Concept maps as facilitative tools in schools and corporations.* Mawah, NJ: Lawrence Erlbaum Associates.

Resnick, L. B. 1983. Mathematics and science learning: A new conception. *Science* 220: 477–78.

Schauble, L. 1990. Belief revision in children: The role of prior knowledge and strategies for generating evidence. *Journal of Experimental Child Psychology* 49: 31–57.

Vosniadou, S., and Brewer, W. F. 1992. Mental models of the Earth: A study of conceptual change in childhood. *Cognitive Psychology* 24: 535–85.

PART 2

Designing Curriculum for Student Learning

Scientific Inquiry, Student Learning, and the Science Curriculum

Rodger W. Bybee

Rodger W. Bybee is the executive director of Biological Sciences Curriculum Study (BSCS). Prior to this, he was executive director of the Center for Science, Mathematics, and Engineering Education at the National Research Council. Author of numerous journal articles and several books, he chaired the content working group of the *National Science Education Standards* and was instrumental in their final development. His honors include the American Institute of Biological Science "Education Award" and the National Science Teachers Association "Distinguished Service Award."

Different disciplines are organized differently and have different approaches to inquiry. For example, the evidence needed to support a set of historical claims is different from the evidence needed to prove a mathematical conjecture, and both of these differ from the evidence needed to test a scientific theory. (Bransford, Brown, and Cocking 1999, 143)

The first sentence of this quotation from *How People Learn: Brain, Mind, Experience, and School* (Bransford, Brown, and Cocking 1999) identifies the major theme of this chapter, which is that the conceptual structures of science disciplines and scientific inquiry should have a prominent place in school science programs. Such a view is consistent with the disciplines of science and supported by contemporary learning theory, but due to complexities such as the culture of schools, high-stakes assessments, and market-driven textbooks, it is not clearly evident in the science curriculum.

Relative to the science curriculum, in this chapter I use the term *scientific inquiry* in three distinct, but complementary ways: as science content that should be understood; as a set of cognitive abilities that students should develop; and as teaching methods that science teachers can use. The views I present here are consistent with those of the *National Science Education Standards* (NRC 1996) and *Inquiry and the National Science Education Standards* (NRC 2000).

The following discussion uses what we now understand about student learning to establish important links between scientific inquiry and the science curriculum. The chapter begins with a discussion of scientific inquiry. I then describe some related ideas from *How People Learn* and apply the discussion of student learning to our understanding of scientific inquiry and to the design of science curricula. I conclude with recommendations for practitioners.

Scientific Inquiry

To understand scientific inquiry and its place in science teaching, let us begin by reviewing some ideas about science and inquiry separately. This discussion sets the stage for later presentations of student learning and the design of science curricula.

Science

The achievements of science provide us interesting and important explanations about the world. Science does not and cannot tell us everything, but it does supply dependable knowledge that helps us understand the world in which we live. Scientific knowledge is greater than an accumulation of facts and information; indeed, it presents ideas and concepts that have explanatory power. That is, scientific knowledge often gives us some understanding of cause-and-effect relationships and the power to predict and control.

Although science supplies reliable knowledge, that knowledge often challenges our everyday ideas about reality. For nonscientists, it may be a challenge to understand that all substances consist of tiny particles held together by electrical forces; that the many materials in our world are made up of different arrangements of a surprisingly small number of particles; that some diseases are caused by microorganisms invisible to the naked eye; that heritable traits result from combinations of a chemical code; that all species have descended from common ancestors; and that huge plates on the Earth's surface are moving in somewhat predictable patterns.

These and other scientific ideas are expressed by terms such as the particulate nature of matter, the germ theory of disease, the genome and DNA, the evolution of life, and plate tectonics. Major ideas such as these and an unimaginable number of other concepts form a body of knowledge called science. Science teachers have the dual challenge of identifying which ideas are most important for students to learn and how to best teach those ideas, given the difference between what students currently know and understand about their world and the accepted scientific explanations about that same world. In educational terms, these two challenges can be summarized as those of curriculum and instruction—specifically, the content of the curriculum and the instructional approaches, strategies, and techniques of presenting that content. But, what about scientific inquiry?

Inquiry

Science is more than a body of knowledge. The concept of science as a way of explaining the world includes knowledge and explanation and the additional idea that science has particular ways or unique methods that scientists use. Indeed, science is more than a body of knowledge; what we know and even what we mean by scientific knowledge is a function of the processes by which scientists come to obtain that knowledge. What, to be specific, are the basic elements of those processes of scientific inquiry? In simple and direct summary, scientific inquiry uses processes such as observations and experiments that result in empirical evidence about the natural world. To be clear, it is not the authority of individuals, the dogma of religions, the doctrines of governments, or the power of private enterprise that carries weight in scientific explanations. Rather, it is the power of empirical evidence, critical analysis, and careful inference derived from observations and experiments that brings authority to scientific explanations. This is the particular and unique way that scientists explain the world.

The prevailing misconception of the public, most textbooks, and, unfortunately, some science teachers is that science is a systematic method that has variations of the following form: first, state a problem; second, form a hypothesis; third, perform an experiment; fourth, analyze data; and finally, present a conclusion. As presented in many science classes, the scientific method is systematic, precise, rigorous, and impersonal (Bauer 1992).

Some observations serve as counterpoints to the misconception of *a* scientific method. At the core of scientific inquiry, one finds observation, hypothesis, inference, test, and feedback. All of these processes serve the end of obtaining and using empirical evidence to help answer a scientific question. The scientist begins with an engaging question based on anomalous data, inconsistencies in a proposed explanation, or insights from observations. After some explorations, the scientist proposes a hypothesis from which predictions may be deduced through inference. Tests are designed to check the validity of the hypothesis. If the tests confirm the hypothesis the results are often published, providing feedback to scientists and the scientific community. Publishing the results is important whether the tests confirm or refute the hypothesis. Both types of feedback are important in science. If the results do not confirm the hypothesis, it may be altered, a new one proposed, or the scientists can stay with the original idea and try another investigation. Although the actual processes are not as clear as just stated, this summary provides insights for teachers and the representation of inquiry in the science curriculum and classroom.

The activity of scientific inquiry is not as tidy as the misconceived scientific method. It is, however, precise and methodologically appropriate to the discipline, the available technology, and the specific question being investigated. Data from the measurements and observations are theory-laden because the original question was guided by the knowledge and concepts of the scientist. After the original statement and testing of the hypothesis, scientists often report their results at a scientific meeting, thus providing initial explanations and methods to the community. Further work elaborates on the original ideas, and subsequent publications provide opportunities for scientists to evaluate the proposed explanation by replicating the original work or applying the explanation to new and different problems. Although ideal, this description at least hints at the complexity and the cyclical nature of scientific inquiry. The processes of observation, hypothesis, inference, test, and feedback continue all the time in a less than tidy manner.

Student Learning

This section establishes linkages between how students learn and scientific inquiry in the curriculum.

Learning Is a Basic, Adaptive Function of Humans

As this heading suggests, early in life, children begin perceiving regularity in objects, organisms, and their environment (Bransford, Brown, and Cocking 1999, xi). They engage in learning—making sense of their world. One can easily infer that children have a predisposition to learn, especially in particular domains such as biological and physical causality, number, space, time, and language. As children attempt to make sense of their world, they form explanations of phenomena that result in initial concepts that go on to form the basis of their scientific understanding of the world.

Learning Originates in Diverse Experiences

Although learning is a basic, adaptive human function and much of what children learn occurs through diverse spontaneous experiences and without formal instruction, when children's explanations are compared with scientific understanding of objects, organisms, and natural phenomena, the learners' explanations are often incomplete, inadequate, or inappropriate. To state the obvious, at some point these children become students, go to schools, and enter science classrooms. Important to this discussion is the fact that these students bring their current conceptions of biological and physical phenomena with them, and, more important, the students' current knowledge influences the learning process. From a science teacher's perspective, students' current knowledge can be viewed as naive, incorrect, or laden with misconceptions.

When students are confronted with new knowledge, they often maintain their current explanations in large part because those conceptions work. From the student's point of view they provide personal explanations of phenomena; in short, current concepts make sense of the world. So, the science teacher is confronted with students' current conceptions that mostly have developed through informal encounters with phenomena and the contrasting conceptions from the scientific body of knowledge. At the heart of this discussion of science teaching and student learning is the idea that new concepts develop from challenges to current conceptions, which may take the form of social interactions, encounters with new and different phenomena, personal reflection, specific questions from peers and parents, activities that are part of the science curriculum, and interactions with science teachers.

How Teachers Can Facilitate Student Learning

Teaching for conceptual change and greater scientific understanding requires systematic approaches designed to identify students' current conceptions; challenge the adequacy of current explanations; introduce scientific concepts that are intelligible, plausible, and helpful; and provide opportunities to apply new ideas in a familiar context.

Students' learning—that is, the formation of better scientific knowledge—may occur through the addition of knowledge to current concepts, creation of new concepts, or major modification of current concepts. In any instance, facilitating student learning requires time and diverse opportunities for students to construct understandings of the world.

Clearly, the contemporary view of how students learn implies content that is deeper than facts and information, a curriculum that is richer than reading, instruction that is longer than a lesson, and teaching that is more than telling. In the next section, I address some of the complex issues of applying a contemporary understanding of student learning to the practical issues of curriculum and instruction.

The Science Curriculum

This section addresses two features of the science curriculum—content and instruction. The discussions complement sections on scientific inquiry and student learning.

Content of the Science Curriculum

Recall the discussion on scientific inquiry. One theme of that discussion was knowledge—specifically, that scientific knowledge presents ideas and concepts in an organized and systematic way. There is, to use Jerome Bruner's phrase from the 1960s, "structure to the disciplines." This theme has a parallel in the research on expert/novice learners. One finding has implications for this discussion. In summarizing the question of how experts' knowledge is organized and how this affects their abilities to understand and represent problems, Bransford, Brown, and Cocking (1999) had this to say:

Their knowledge is not simply a list of facts and formulas that are relevant to their domain; instead, their knowledge is organized around core concepts or "big ideas" that guide their thinking about their domains. (24)

Most science curricula used in K–12 education tend to overemphasize facts and information while underemphasizing major concepts and "big ideas." The *National Science Education Standards* (NRC 1996) provide one example of a set of recommendations that would emphasize major conceptual ideas and fundamental concepts associated with those ideas for grades K–4, 5–8, and 9–12. One also should note that the recommendation to emphasize major concepts is consistent with findings from the Third International Mathematics and Science Study (TIMSS) (Schmidt, McKnight, and Raizen 1997; Schmidt et al. 1999).

Organization of Content

Although the *National Science Education Standards* (NRC 1996) do *not* represent a curriculum, the content standards illustrate important features such as emphasis on major ideas, links to meaningful experiences, and uses that are developmentally appropriate for the learner. For example, Table 1 illustrates content standards that might be used as major conceptual organizers in a science curriculum.

Table 1. Major Conceptual Organizers from the *National Science Education Standards*

	Grades K–4	Grades 5–8	Grades 9–12
Physical Science (matter)	Properties of objects and materials	Properties and changes of properties of matter	Structure of atoms Structure and properties of matter
(energy)	Light, heat, electricity, and magnetism	Transfer of energy	Conservation of energy and increase in disorders
Life Science (evolution)	Characteristics of organisms	Diversity and adaptations of organisms	Biological evolution
(genetics)	Life cycles of organisms	Reproduction and heredity	Molecular basis of heredity
Earth/Space Sciences (Earth systems)	Properties of Earth materials	Structures of the Earth system	Origin and evolution of the Earth system
(astronomy)	Objects in the sky	Earth in the solar system	Origin and evolution of the universe

The organization of content illustrated in Table 1 would support learning for understanding and making sense of experiences. This "progressive formalization" begins with the informal ideas that students bring to school in the lower grades (K–4) and gradually helps them develop and perhaps restructure those ideas into formal science concepts in the upper grades (9–12). Content in a curriculum would be organized so students build scientific understanding and abilities of inquiry in a gradual and structured manner during their school years.

Use of the *National Science Education Standards* and the organization of content, such as just illustrated, reduces the emphasis on facts, increases the emphasis on major ideas, and provides focus, coherence, and rigor to the science curriculum. From a larger view of school science programs, it gives students time to confront and reconstruct concepts that form the structure of science disciplines. This approach aligns with prior discussions of a knowledge base for scientific inquiry, is supported from the perspective of student learning, and provides a positive response to criticisms that the U.S. science curriculum lacks focus, coherence, and rigor (Schmidt, McKnight, and Raizen 1997; NRC 1999).

I conclude this section by pointing out that some curriculum materials that align with the aforementioned characteristics do exist, although they are not widely used. For example, the BSCS program *BSCS Science T.R.A.C.S.* at the elementary level and *BSCS Biology: A Human Approach* for high school life sciences are two such programs. Other National Science Foundation (NSF)–supported programs such as *Active Physics, Chemistry in the Community,* and *Earth Science in the Community* also align with national standards. (See *Profiles in Science: A Guide to NSF-Funded High School Instructional Materials*, BSCS 2001).

Effective Science Instruction

Science teaching is a complex process that, at best, combines an understanding of students, science, and the educational environment as teachers make long-term decisions about the curriculum and instantaneous responses to classroom situations. This complexity notwithstanding, based on the results of research on learning, there are some understandings and practices that will make science instruction more effective.

An Instructional Model

Children's curiosity leads to their informed inquiries into many aspects of the world. The natural inquiry of children and the more formal problem solving of adults often follow a pattern of initial engagement, exploration of alternatives, formation of an explanation, use of the explanation, and evaluation of the explanation based on its efficacy and responses from others. I will note here that this process of natural inquiry is quite similar to the more formal processes of scientific inquiry, as described in prior sections. The parallel is intended, and in fact, extends to the discussion of student learning. I quote from a section on knowledge-centered environments in *How People Learn.*

> *An alternative to simply progressing through a series of exercises that derive from a scope and sequence chart is to expose students to the major features of a subject domain as they arise naturally in problem situations. Activities can be structured so that students are able to explore, explain, extend, and evaluate their progress. Ideas are best introduced when students see a need or a reason for their use—this helps them see relevant uses of knowledge to make sense of what they are learning.* (Bransford, Brown, and Cocking 1999, 127)

This quotation directs our attention to the research-based recommendation that activities be structured to allow students to explore, explain, extend, and evaluate their progress. Note the suggestion that activities are structured to encourage conceptual change and a progressive re-forming of their ideas. This structured approach to teaching is further justified by the fact that the opportunities and time allow students to see relevant uses and make sense of their learning experiences. This discussion leads to support for an instructional model, specifically the BSCS 5E model I have advocated for over two decades (see, e.g., the structure of chapters in Bybee and Sund 1982; Chapter 8, "Improving Instruction," in Bybee 1997). Since the late 1980s the 5E model also has been used extensively in BSCS programs. Table 2 summarizes the 5E model.

Table 2. The BSCS 5E Instructional Model

ENGAGE

Engage lessons provide the opportunity for science teachers to identify students' current concepts and misconceptions. Although provided by a teacher or structured by curriculum materials, these activities introduce major ideas of science in problem situations. The theme here might be—*how do I explain this situation?*

EXPLORE

Explore lessons provide a common set of experiences for students and opportunities for them to "test" their ideas with their own experiences and those of peers and the science teacher. The theme for this phase is—*how do my exploration and explanation of experiences compare with others?* Students have the opportunity to compare ideas that identify inadequacies of current concepts. Here, the theme is—*how does one challenge misconceptions?*

EXPLAIN

Explain lessons provide opportunities for students to use their previous experiences to recognize misconceptions and to begin making conceptual sense of the activities through the construction of new ideas and understandings. This stage also allows for the introduction of formal language, scientific terms, and content information that makes students' previous experiences easier to describe and explain. The theme is—*this is a scientific explanation.*

ELABORATE

Elaborate lessons apply or extend the student's developing concepts in new activities and relate their previous experiences to the current activities. Now the theme is—*how does the new explanation work in a different situation?*

EVALUATE

Evaluate lessons can serve as a summative assessment of what students know and can do at this point. Students confront a new activity that requires the understandings and abilities developed in previous activities. The final theme is—*how do students understand and apply scientific concepts and abilities?*

The BSCS 5E model was initially based on and elaborated earlier instructional approaches (Bybee 1997). It was designed as an instructional sequence primarily for use at the activity level. Although not originally based on scientific inquiry as discussed earlier, general connections seem evident. Likewise, connections with classroom inquiry and the general theme of teaching science as inquiry appear to be clear.

Linking Inquiry and Instruction

The BSCS 5E model takes a curricular perspective, in particular a view that incorporates what we know about how students learn and accommodates many everyday requirements of science teaching. For example, the instructional model can be used

Table 3. Essential Features of Classroom Inquiry and Their Variations along Two Continua

Essential Feature	Amount of Learner Self-Direction ———— More ⟶ Less Amount of Direction from Teacher or Written Material ———— Less ⟶ More			
Learner **engages** in scientifically oriented questions	Learner poses a question	Learner selects among questions, poses new questions	Learner sharpens or clarifies question provided by teacher, materials, or other source	Learner engages in question provided by teacher, materials, or other source
Learner gives priority to **evidence** in responding to questions	Learner determines what constitutes evidence and collects it	Learner directed to collect certain data	Learner given data and asked to analyze	Learner given data and told how to analyze
Learner formulates **explanations** from evidence	Learner formulates explanation after summarizing evidence	Learner guided in process of formulating explanations from evidence	Learner given possible ways to use evidence to formulate explanation	Learner provided with evidence
Learner connects explanations to scientific **knowledge**	Learner independently examines other resources and forms the links to explanations	Learner directed toward areas and sources of scientific knowledge	Learner given possible connections	Learner given steps and procedures for communication
Learner **communicates** and **justifies** explanations	Learner forms reasonable and logical argument to communicate explanations	Learner coached in development of communication	Learner provided broad guidelines to use to sharpen communication	Learner given connections to scientific knowledge

Adapted from National Research Council (NRC). 2000. *Inquiry and the National Science Education Standards.* Washington, DC: National Academy Press.

with thirty or more students; it also incorporates laboratory investigations, educational technology, cooperative learning, and other strategies. Classroom inquiry has five essential features as described in *Inquiry and the National Science Education Standards* (NRC 2000). Those features are summarized as follows:

1. Learners ENGAGE in scientifically oriented questions.

2. Learners give priority to EVIDENCE in responding to questions.

3. Learners formulate EXPLANATIONS from evidence.

4. Learners connect explanations to scientific KNOWLEDGE.

5. Learners COMMUNICATE and JUSTIFY explanations.

Although not a direct and a one-to-one correspondence, the connections among scientific inquiry, student learning, and the 5E model should be evident. Table 3 presents these essential features and variations of the features as they may appear in science classrooms.

From the perspective of teacher direction and student self-direction, few, if any, students will demonstrate the essential features of inquiry when they first experience scientific investigations. Because of this, science teachers will find practical value and support for their work in the variations of these essential features as they implement a curriculum, teach science as inquiry, and work toward a professional goal to further students' understanding of science.

Conclusion

This chapter uses student learning, specifically the National Research Council's report *How People Learn*, as a bridge connecting scientific inquiry and curriculum with instruction in science. Use of content standards from the *National Science Education Standards* and the 5E instructional model were presented as practical ways for science teachers to incorporate scientific inquiry and apply our understanding of student learning. Teaching science as inquiry provides opportunities for students to learn fundamental concepts, develop the abilities of inquiry, and acquire an understanding of science.

Specifically, the following recommendations emerge from this chapter. Practitioners will establish connections between scientific inquiry and enhance student learning when they:

◆ Focus on core content, for example, the fundamental concepts articulated in the *National Science Education Standards*.

◆ Use an instructional sequence that supports what we know about student learning, for example, the BSCS 5E model.

◆ Create knowledge-centered learning environments that incorporate the essential features of classroom inquiry, for example, those described in *Inquiry and the National Science Education Standards* (NRC 2000).

References

Bauer, H. H. 1992. *Scientific literacy and the myth of the scientific method*. Chicago, IL: University of Illinois Press.

Bransford, J., Brown, A., and Cocking, R., eds. 1999. *How people learn: Brain, mind, experience, and school*. Washington, DC: National Academy Press.

BSCS (The SCI Center). 2001. *Profiles in science: A guide to NSF-funded high school instructional materials*. Colorado Springs, CO: BSCS.

Bybee, R. 1997. *Achieving scientific literacy: From purposes to practices*. Portsmouth, NH: Heinemann.

Bybee, R., and Sund, R. 1982. *Piaget for educators*. Columbus, OH: Charles E. Merrill.

National Research Council (NRC). 1996. *National science education standards*. Washington, DC: National Academy Press.

———. 1999. *Global perspectives for local action: Using TIMSS to improve U.S. mathematics and science education*. Washington, DC: National Academy Press.

———. 2000. *Inquiry and the national science education standards: A guide for teaching and learning*. Washington, DC: National Academy Press.

Schmidt, W. H., McKnight, C. C., and Raizen, S .A. 1997. *Splintered vision: An investigation of U.S. science and mathematics education*. Boston: Kluwer Academic.

Schmidt, W. H., McKnight, C. C., Cogan, L. S., Jakwerth, P. M., and Houang, R. T. 1999. *Facing the consequences: Using TIMSS for a closer look at U.S. mathematics and science education*. Boston, MA: Kluwer Academic.

Supporting the Science-Literacy Connection

Jeanne Rose Century, Joseph Flynn, Doris Santamaria Makang, Marian Pasquale,
Karen M. Robblee, Jeffrey Winokur, and Karen Worth

Jeanne Rose Century is a senior project director in the Center for Science Education at Education Development Center, Inc. (EDC). Her past work at EDC includes development of the *Insights* curriculum and provision of technical assistance to school districts implementing systemic elementary science education programs. She currently directs several National Science Foundation–funded research and evaluation projects that focus on issues such as sustainability of reform, rural districts' participation in reform opportunities, the impact of inquiry strategies, instructional strategies that lead to high achievement in both science and reading, and the relationship between curriculum implementation and student outcomes. She was recently a fellow with the National Institute for Science Education at the University of Wisconsin in Madison.

Joseph (Joe) Flynn taught middle school science in Cleveland, researched policy positions on science and vocational education for a statewide education advocacy organization, developed a community-based collaborative for secondary science education reform, and managed a program for systemic reform of elementary science. At the Center for Science Education at Education Development Center, Inc. (EDC), he provides technical assistance to school districts that are reforming their science programs and directs the Foundation Science curriculum-development project.

Doris Santamaria Makang is a research associate at the Center for Science Education at Education Development Center, Inc. (EDC). Previously she worked as a high school teacher with the Boston Public School System in regular and the bilingual programs. At EDC, she provides technical assistance to school districts involved in improving their K-12 science programs. As a member of the K-12 Science Curriculum Dissemination Center team, she focused on reviewing and developing profiles for curriculum materials. She is co-author of EDC's Middle School Science Curriculum Guide, and is a member of Project 2061's Literacy Leaders in Math and Science at the American Association for the Advancement of Science. She is a native of Colombia, South America, where she taught in high school and college; at the latter, she taught courses for prospective secondary science teachers.

Marian Pasquale served as a middle school teacher and curriculum coordinator for twenty years in Haverill, Massachusetts. Since 1992 she has been a senior research and development associate at the Center for Science Education, Education Development Center, Inc. (EDC), where she leads the middle-grades team. She is currently co-principal investigator of an effort funded by the National Science Foundation to develop a model middle grades science mentoring program. She recently co-authored *Guiding Curriculum Decisions for Middle Grades Science*, a publication prepared under a grant from the Edna McConnell Clark Foundation and the W. K. Kellogg Foundation. She has co-authored an article entitled, "Providing School and District Level Support for Science Education Reform," for *Science Educator* (in press).

Karen M. Robblee is an instructional specialist in mathematics and science for the Franklin, Massachusetts, School System. Her prior experiences include positions as senior research associate at Education Development Center, Inc. (EDC), curriculum developer for educational publishing houses, and classroom teacher. She is co-author of *Chemistry: Connections to Our Changing World*. She has also presented workshops on writing across the curriculum, laboratory safety, and the use of interactive visualization models in teaching science.

Jeffrey Winokur is a senior research associate currently working on the Tool Kit for Early Childhood Science and the K-12 Science Curriculum Dissemination Center at the Center for Science Education at Education Development Center, Inc. (EDC). He is also an early childhood and elementary science specialist at Wheelock College, where he teaches both undergraduate and graduate level courses in the teaching of science to children ages 3–12. He has served as staff developer on a project that developed science training materials for preschool settings and as Wheelock's liaison to the Boston Public Schools for the Massachusetts State Systemic Initiative.

Karen Worth is a senior scientist at Education Development Center, Inc. (EDC) and faculty member in the Graduate School of Education at Wheelock College. She has directed a number of major science education reform projects, including the development of *Insights*, an elementary hands-on, inquiry-based science curriculum. She chaired the teaching and professional development working group of the *National Science Education Standards* and serves on a number of advisory boards for major science education reform projects across the country.

This chapter explores the mutual roles of language and science skills in the learning environment, and the reciprocal benefits of developing those skills together. Specifically, it focuses on how effective language skills contribute to making students' science thinking more "visible." The emphasis is on the formative years of language and thinking development in the elementary grades. That discussion is followed by a brief consideration of the connections between language and science in the secondary grades.

Mary Rizzuto teaches at the Tobin Elementary School in Cambridge, Massachusetts. She teaches the same children through grades one and two. Eric Carle's book *The Very Hungry Caterpillar* (1969) appears in Mary's classroom in grade one among many picture books available to children as they learn to read. It is also used as a "read-aloud" book because of its engaging story and wonderful illustrations.

Near the end of the science unit on life cycles in the second grade, *The Very Hungry Caterpillar* reappears. The second graders have observed and described the life cycles of several animals: mealworms, silkworms, frogs, and painted lady butterflies. The class is brought together, each child with a small clipboard, paper, and pencil. They are divided into two groups, one group instructed to listen carefully for evidence of what the author knows about butterflies, the other group instructed to listen for evidence of what the author doesn't know about butterflies. Mary then reads the book as the children take notes. At the end of the reading, the children share and record their observations, such as, "The author knows that the caterpillar grows and changes," and, "He left out that the caterpillar molts as it grows."

Mary follows this experience on another day by reading Heiligman's *From Caterpillar to Butterfly* (1996). As they listen, children find ample evidence of what this author knows about butterflies, and little or no evidence of what she doesn't know. Mary uses these experiences as opportunities for children to think critically about text and to value their own experiences and ideas.

Mary Rizutto's strategic instruction enriches her students' learning in reading, writing, and science. She does this in the face of the national challenge to find a place for science while the emphasis on literacy is so dominant.

One would hope that all teachers could have the support and knowledge necessary to bring science alive for their students in such a creative and meaningful way. But in today's environment of high-stakes tests and increased accountability for student performance, elementary teachers are under pressure to devote more and more classroom time to reading and mathematics—the subject areas that receive the most public and media attention and are most visible in the political discourse. As a result, language arts and science are perceived as competing for classroom time and attention, and science is often neglected. As one science coordinator remarked, "Literacy is taking over elementary grades—how can we sustain science in this atmosphere?" The impact of this issue is felt in middle and high school as well.

Regrettably, at all grade levels, teachers of students who perform poorly on literacy-related standardized tests are particularly susceptible to the pressures to improve students' scores. In some cases, elementary teachers are even instructed by their supervisors to teach nothing but the "basics," denying their students science instruction altogether. Despite demands for accountability and equal opportunity for all students, opportunities for science learning are fading. As a result, efforts to identify and establish the mutually beneficial linkages between high-quality instruction in science and literacy are particularly timely.

Linking Literacy and Science

Effective literacy instruction need not be at the expense of meaningful science instruction. Language arts and science instruction naturally support one another. The *National Science Education Standards (NSES)* (NRC 1996) state that "Students in school science programs should develop the abilities associated with accurate and effective communication. These include writing and following procedures, expressing concepts, reviewing information, summarizing data, using language appropriately,…constructing a reasoned argument, and responding appropriately to critical comments" (176). Similarly, the National Council of Teachers of English's guidelines entitled *Elementary School Practices* (1993) encourage purposeful use of language, such as the use of language skills in the exploration and study of science. The guidelines explain that "children learn best when they are working on meaningful projects—actively involved in experiments or explorations on a range of topics that interest them."

Many researchers have explored the practical application of these guidelines. Their investigations include a consideration of the interaction between science and language skills. The focus of the reports, however, varies:

◆ The integration of reading and science instruction generally (Flick 1995; Romance and Vitale 1992; Morrow, Pressley, Smith, and Smith 1997),

◆ Integration of reading and hands-on science in particular (Scarnati and Weller 1992; Bristor 1994),

◆ Writing and reading as tools to improve science instruction (Fogarty 1991; Harmelink 1998; Jacobs 1989; Stotsky 1984; Holliday, Yore, and Alvermann 1994),

◆ Writing, concept mapping, and other strategies to help students develop understanding and to inform teachers about the state of that understanding (Gallagher 1993), and

◆ Writing performance by students in inquiry-based settings (Klentchy, Garrison, and Amaral 2000).

The potentially powerful linkages between science and literacy also are supported by research on cognition, recently synthesized in the National Research Council's *How People Learn: Brain, Mind, Experience, and School* (Bransford, Brown, and Cocking 2000). Literacy skill development cannot be disconnected from the substance of the reading and writing. "The knowledge-acquisition strategies the students learn in working on a specific text are not acquired as abstract memorized procedures, but as skills instrumental in achieving subject-area knowledge and understanding" (55). Furthermore, second-language acquisition is most successful when the focus of instruction is on substance rather than on form, and there is sufficient opportunity to engage in meaningful use of that language (Krashen 1982; Crandall 1994; Baker and Saul 1994; Gallas 1995). As students communicate, they learn to clarify, refine, and consolidate their thinking. "When students have to explain, argue, and reflect on their work rather than simply select responses, answer questions, and complete standard form assignments, both their writing and inquiry skills are enhanced" (Shymansky, Marberry, and Jorgensen 1977, 4). Through scientific inquiry, students have opportunities to use language in the context of solving meaningful problems, and as a result, engage in the kind of purposeful communicative interactions that promote genuine language use (Trueba, Guthrie, and Au 1981).

The benefits of incorporating language and science learning also extend to formal and informal oral speech, including discussion and dialogue (Beck 1968). Informal discourse provides students with a forum for exploring their own ideas and considering those of their peers. More formal presentations are opportunities for students to organize and defend their thoughts and ideas. Discussion, questioning, and debate allow students to clarify their thinking and experience the type of discourse that occurs in the scientific community (Hodson 1998). Furthermore, "in addition to its role in facilitating understanding, collaborative talk between teacher and students...empowers students by negotiating a transfer of responsibility. It encourages and supports students in taking increasing responsibility for aspects of the particular task in-hand and eventually, for learning and inquiry in general" (Hodson and Hodson 1998, 22).

Scientific and reading processes develop simultaneously because science process skills have reading counterparts (Koballa and Bethe 1984). Also, science programs provide opportunities for development of expository reading and writing for students who otherwise learn language skills primarily through narrative work. When teachers help students analyze the language and layout of the exposition, they enhance general reading, comprehension, and critical-thinking skills (Hodson and Hodson 1998).

Implications for Elementary School Practice

In light of limited time and resources, elementary school teachers need research-grounded strategies for providing high-quality instruction in science and language arts. We face the challenge of demonstrating how high-quality science can become part of the core, mainstream instructional experience for all students and how educators can increase students' literacy abilities while engaging them in important, rigorous studies of science. Both research and practical experience demonstrate that language is an essential part of science learning and that both native English speakers and English Language Learners develop their language skills through authentic experiences.

All approaches to science instruction require language. In programs focused on the acquisition of facts and information, students read from science texts, answer questions in writing, prepare research reports on various topics, and write structured lab reports. However, the renewed emphasis on inquiry-based science education opens the door for richer use of language and opportunities to establish more powerful relationships between the two domains.

Curriculum development of the past decade, based in the vision of the standards and emerging research, has generated a number of unit-based or modular curricula that shift the emphasis of instruction toward student inquiry and investigation. Some might argue that too great an emphasis on investigation risks denying students opportunities to develop skills in critical reading and written and oral communication. But initial efforts to integrate literacy into modular curricula (including use of aligned trade books, open-ended worksheets, portfolios of student work and student journals, and structured discussions and presentations) suggest there is great potential in this kind of science instruction for literacy development. However, this potential will only be reached "through providing students with opportunities to read, write, and speak as scientists; attaching purpose to the use of print materials; and making the conventions and forms of reading, writing, and speaking in science explicit" (DiGisi 1998, 3). In other words, thoughtful, structured, intentional use of language must be an integral part of the science curriculum (Ruiz-Primo, Li, and Shavelson 2001; Cutter, Vincent, Palincsar, and Magnusson 2001).

One framework for bringing structure to the use of language in elementary science builds on identifying when opportunities for development of particular language skills are in the foreground during the inquiry process. With such a framework in mind, elementary teachers can provide the resources for, and explicit instruction in, literacy skills at the appropriate time. Table 1 provides such a framework. In it we draw from the inquiry standard of the *National Science Education Standards* (NRC 1996) to define inquiry as a process for developing understanding that has four components or stages: engagement and exploration, design and conduct of scientific investigations, analysis and interpretation of data, and presentation of findings and understanding. Each of these stages uses reading, writing, speaking, and listening for specific purposes and, therefore, requires customized strategies for language instruction.

In the first stage, students experience a phenomenon or confront a challenge for the first time. Discussion and sharing within small groups is likely to be informal and focused on early wondering, surprise, questions, and connections to past experiences. While the emphasis in this stage is on direct experience, reading may still play a supportive role and inspire new questions and motivate further exploration. Similarly, writing in a science notebook can support exploration through jotting brief notes, recording impressions, and describing phenomena.

Building from this open exploration to the second stage, students arrive at a question they wish to explore, or the teacher may gently guide them to a specific query. As students design and conduct their investigations, informal language use in cooperative groups and jotted notes and questions continue, but the necessity arises for more formal use of language. Scientific experimentation requires careful recording of procedure and data so that students can conduct their analyses and replicate experiences. As investigations move forward, carefully selected books provide needed information, examples of experimentation, and new experimental strategies. Group discussions still include impressions and feelings, but must also focus on the clear sharing of data and the beginning of thoughtful analysis.

Then, as students start to analyze and interpret their data in the third stage, they must learn to draw from the data recorded in their notebooks and generate beginning findings based on the evidence. They must write clear descriptions of their analyses as well as initial explanations of their conclusions. Students also engage with oral language focused on the study of data in large and small groups and thoughtful presentations of ideas with careful explanations and rational arguments. Books may serve the purpose of filling in missing pieces of information and be sources for supporting or questioning tentative conclusions.

Finally, the work in any unit must come to closure. At this fourth stage, writing in notebooks and discussions reflect the most reasonable syntheses of data and conclusions drawn from individual and group experience. Then, findings are formalized in a report, presentation, and/or publication that is clear and honed—the final product of the work. This, then, is a time to study the work of others: their style of presentation, models, and their conclusions.

Table 1. Science Inquiry and Literacy

Stages of Inquiry*	Writing	Reading	Speaking and Listening
1. Engage and Explore · wonder · notice · interact with organisms, objects, and phenomena	Purposes · think · reflect Types of writing · note taking · descriptive · speculative	Purposes · inspire · raise questions · enrich Types of books · fictional reality · wonder · personal experiences · biographies	Purposes · share ideas and wonder · generate questions · build vocabulary Types of settings · small-group discussion · one-on-one · informal large-group discussions
2. Design and Conduct Scientific Investigations · identify question · plan and implement an investigation · observe systematically · gather and organize data	Purposes · document process and data · save emerging thoughts Types of writing · procedural · data display · descriptive · technical · graphic	Purposes · provide examples of investigations · extend experience · provide information and vocabulary Types of books · experiment · field guide · information	Purposes · discuss strategies and ideas · clarify procedures and data collection · listen to others' ideas
3. Analyze and Interpret Data · identify patterns and relationships · develop descriptions, explanations, models, and predictions using evidence	Purposes · clarify thinking · communicate ideas · raise new questions Types of writing · analytic and interpretive · descriptive, explanatory model building · predictive · reflective	Purposes · support and validate ideas · provide information · raise new questions Types of books · information · reports · scientific notebooks	Purposes · organize thinking · argue based on evidence · reflect on data Types of settings · small-group analysis · small- and large-group presentation and discussion
4. Present Findings and Understandings · organize findings and understandings · develop report using a variety of media · present, publish, report	Purposes · communicate clearly to others Types of writing · reporting · formal	Purposes · exemplify writing styles and presentation strategies · provide alternative models Types of books · information · scientific report · text	Purposes · communicate formally · listen and argue clearly Types of settings · formal presentation · debate

* Drawn from National Research Council (NRC). 1996. *National Science Education Standards*. Washington, DC: National Academy Press.

The portrayal of Kathy Hernandez's classroom below brings this framework to life and demonstrates how it translates to practical classroom practice.

Kathy Hernandez's grade four children at an elementary school in Ohio engage in Writers' Workshop five days per week. Science journals are a staple in Kathy's classroom. Several years ago these two experiences were separate, but Kathy now frequently combines the two writing experiences and devotes some of the Writers' Workshop time to encouraging children to think about and work on their science writing. Writing at Inquiry Stage 1 promotes students' initial thinking and speculation about the science to come while it stimulates further the wonder that is emerging.

In the midst of a recent soils unit, children spent much of their science time in hands-on exploration and experimentation with different soil types. They planted cucumber seeds in a variety of media, including sand, clay, and humus. As they set up their experiments and observed the seeds over several weeks, the children recorded their procedures, observations, and other data in the three-ring binders they use as science journals. The focus was on description: color, shape, size, and change over time. Kathy expects an informal writing style in this situation. She is less focused here on spelling, appropriate capitalization, or complete sentences than on encouraging children to capture their observations using descriptive words or phrases. At this Inquiry Stage 2, students question, plan, observe, and gather data, a process made more careful by the writing that documents and describes their work and their findings.

During Writers' Workshop Kathy asked children to use special science notebooks and expand on the observations and descriptions they made during science time. The children used these notebooks to write their analyses of the data and emerging conclusions, ideas, and new questions. Kathy posed specific questions on the board: "What surprised you about what you observed and why?" and "What do you think was happening?" In describing the process, Kathy said, "It is through the writing process that children get their thinking out on paper. I have children whose writing is otherwise basic but who love to sit and write about their science experiences. Science writing is like a template for them; they know where to start and where to go, and even write about what they find surprising and why." The explanatory and reflective writing is advancing Inquiry Stage 3 analysis and interpretation of the students' findings.

Kathy has noticed that her approaches to teaching both science and writing have grown together over the past several years. When her school system first implemented a hands-on, inquiry-based approach to science teaching, she felt it was enough to collect all of a child's records in one three-ring binder, a "multi-purpose science journal." However, she began to realize that this rarely pushed children to use their data and put their thinking into clear writing. The three-ring binder for informal note taking during science time and the composition notebook for expanding children's thinking and more formal writing provide children with much clearer and more explicit guidance in the use of writing in science. As the science experience concludes with Inquiry Stage 4, students are communicating to each other the whole of their work from original question to ultimate conclusion.

The uses of language described in Table 1 will enhance science and language learning only if, like Kathy Hernandez, the teacher explicitly teaches the skills and responds actively as students use them. If student notebooks contain fragmented data or incorrect information, they are of little use for reflection or communication. If students copy information from books, the web, or the board, they may have little understanding of what they have read. If books are not used critically, students may not appreciate the nature of scientific debate and the value of their own experiences. If discussion does not move beyond sharing to thoughtful presentation, active listening, debate, and argument, it serves little purpose. At each stage, the teacher's role is critical.

Implications for Middle School and Beyond

Just as in earlier grades, at the middle and high school levels, literacy improves through appropriate science instruction while science learning is enhanced by strong literacy skills. For many years, reading has traditionally been an integral part of middle school science programs, with textbooks as the primary source. Even when teachers use modular materials, they often use a textbook to some degree and for varying purposes, no matter how old that textbook might be. For example, they might use a book to enhance students' expository reading ability, to provide necessary background for student investigations and use of inquiry-type materials, and to learn vocabulary and content required for district and state science tests. As middle school teachers consider the use of language in science instruction, they need to determine the most appropriate purposes for reading and writing in science, the best uses of the text in the overall program, and how reading and writing can contribute to inquiry teaching and learning. The following vignette is one illustration of such thoughtful use:

Karen Spaulding teaches eighth-grade science in Cambridge, Massachusetts. While the majority of her program engages students in hands-on, inquiry experiences, she believes that reading plays a vital role in students' conceptual development. She asks her students to read for various reasons—to obtain information, to acquire vocabulary related to concepts, and to cultivate the scientific language necessary to explain concepts.

In a recent unit on bio-diversity, students designed and built a bug-collecting device, collected as many different insects as possible from a 2 m square plot, and then made careful observations about the individual insects and the collection as a whole. Surprised by the variation among their collections, the students began asking questions. Karen asked them to record their questions in a notebook that was eventually compiled into a class list, ultimately leading to some carefully structured research about diversity of species using text materials.

Recognizing that her middle grades students did not have solid research skills, Karen gave each student Post-It notes for note-taking purposes. As they read, she instructed them to jot down what they believed to be important ideas, the related vocabulary, and any questions they had about what they read. Classification was next. Karen told students to create a concept web about what they had read, which helped them look at their collections again and identify patterns. Students began sorting and eventually created a class key for the insects they had collected. At this point, it was a simple step to understanding and using a dichotomous key.

In reflecting on their work, Karen said, "I'm amazed at how excited the kids get with their bug collecting and how much they want to read and research what they've found." But she also knows that the quality of the reading and research depends on her careful instruction in the necessary skills. The sequence from "engagement" to "understanding" (Table 1) guides her process of instruction, as it can for all K–12 teachers of science.

New understandings about how students learn science also influence the choices high school science teachers make in their instructional strategies. An important part of teaching students through active engagement with natural phenomena is facilitating their understanding and application of the related scientific ideas. In the process, the teacher must continually assess student abilities, alternative conceptions, and depth of understanding. Such a process requires opportunities for students to communicate with their teachers and peers.

Also, teachers who appreciate the reciprocal development of language skills and scientific understanding will provide more opportunities and guidance for students to pursue reading, writing, and discussion as vehicles through which they acquire and refine their knowledge. Such teachers recognize that the two sets of skills develop at the same time. Although language development may not be traditionally seen as a learning outcome or teaching goal of high school science, the high school science program will of necessity either foster it or impede it, and in so doing, foster or impede students' scientific understanding.

Researchers have examined various language-based strategies for development of scientific understanding that begins with direct experience (Gallagher 1993; Keyes, et al. 1999; Hodson 1998). The techniques include:

◆ reading from scientific journals, the popular press, and the Internet;

◆ writing of individual student scientific journals with reflections on classroom or laboratory experiences;

◆ collaborative writing about the scientific work of a group of students;

◆ laboratory notebooks using templates that guide student thinking and elicit critical evaluation of evidence that supports their own or others' scientific claims;

◆ informal discourse among students for the peer exploration of original ideas;

◆ formal individual or group presentations of well-organized and well-defended thinking; and

◆ discussion, questioning, and debate that stimulates clarification of thinking and simulates the discourse that occurs in the scientific community.

When high school science teachers help students develop facility with language, the students also develop the capacity for scientific understanding. A sure way to develop scientific understanding is also to develop powers of language.

In Summary

As one considers the relationship between literacy and science at each age level, a common theme appears. While the emphasis on this relationship does challenge the teacher to step outside of common practice, the result is a learning experience for the children that echoes the daily experience of making sense of our world. We take in information from many different sources; consider which information to use and which to ignore; and mesh and consolidate that information so that we can develop meaningful understandings. As the teachers in the vignettes show us, helping students develop the skills to make these linkages in the classroom enriches their experience both in and outside of the school. Hodson (1998) summarizes the issue well: "It is through the combination of talking, reading, writing, and doing science, and their interaction, that students are stimulated to reflect on these processes, on their learning and its development, and on the nature of science itself"(166).

References

Baker, L., and Saul, E. W. 1994. Considering science and language arts connections: A study of teacher cognition. *Journal of Research in Science Teaching* 31(9): 1023-1037.

Beck, I. 1968. Improving practice through understanding reading. In L. B. Resnick and L. E. Klopfer, eds., *Toward the thinking curriculum: Current cognitive research,* 40–58. Washington, DC: Association for Supervision and Curriculum Development.

Bransford, J. D., Brown, A. L., and Cocking, R. R., eds. 2000. *How people learn: Brain, mind, experience, and school.* Expanded Edition. Washington, DC: National Academy Press.

Bristor, V. 1994. Combining reading and writing with science to enhance content area achievement and attitudes. *Reading Horizons* 35 (1): 30–43.

Carle, E. 1969. *The very hungry caterpillar*. New York: Philomel Books

Crandall, J. 1994. Content-centered language learning. ERIC Digest. ERIC Clearinghouse on Languages and Linguistics. [Online]. Available: *www.cal.org/ericcll/digest/cranda01.html*.

Cutter, J., Vincent, M., Palincsar, A., and Magnusson, S. 2001. The cases of the black felt and missing light: Examining classroom discourse for evidence of learning with an innovative genre of science text. Paper presented at the Annual Meeting of the American Educational Research Association, 10–14 April, Seattle.

DiGisi, L. L. 1998. Summary of CUSER Institute on Science and Literacy. Unpublished paper for Education Development Center, Inc., Newton, MA. [Online]. Available: *www2.edc.org/cse/pdfs/products/literacy.pdf*.

Flick, L. B. 1995. Complex instruction in complex classrooms: A synthesis of research on inquiry teaching methods and explicit teaching strategies. Paper presented at the Annual Meeting of the National Association for Research in Science Teaching, 22–25 April, San Francisco.

Fogarty, R. 1991. Ten ways to integrate curriculum. *Educational Leadership* 49 (2): 61–65.

Gallagher, J. J. 1993. Secondary science teachers and constructivist practice. In K. Tobin, ed., *The practice of constructivism in science education,* 181–92. Hillsdale, NJ: Lawrence Erlbaum Associates.

Gallas, K. 1995. *Talking their way into science*. New York: Teachers College Press.

Harmelink, K. 1998. Learning the write way. *Science Teacher* 65 (1): 36–38.

Heiligman, D., and Weissman, B. (illustrator). 1996. *From caterpillar to butterfly*. New York: Harper Collins Children's Books.

Hodson, D. 1998. Teaching and learning science: Towards a personalized approach. *Online School Science Review*. [Online]. Available: *www.ase.org.uk/publish/jnews/ssr/hodsonsep98.html*

Hodson, D., and Hodson, J. 1998. Science education as enculturation: Some implications for practice. *School Science Review* 80 (290): 17–24.

Holliday, W., Yore, L., and Alvermann, C. 1994. The reading-science learning-writing connection: Breakthroughs, barriers, and promises. *Journal of Research in Science Teaching* 31 (9): 877–93.

Jacobs, H. H. 1989. *Interdisciplinary curriculum: Design and implementation*. Alexandria, VA: Association for Supervision and Curriculum Development.

Keyes, C. W., Hand, B., Prain, V., and Collins, S. 1999. Using the science writing heuristic as a tool for learning from laboratory investigations in secondary science. *Journal of Research in Science Teaching* 36 (10): 1065–1084.

Klentchy, M., Garrison, L., and Amaral, O. M. 2000. Valle Imperial project in science: Four-year comparison of student achievement data, 1995–1999. Unpublished paper.

Koballa, Jr., T. R., and Bethe, L. J. 1984. Integration of science and other school subjects. In D. Holdzkom and P. B. Lutz, eds., *Research within reach: Science education,* 79–108. Washington, DC: National Science Teachers Association.

Krashen, S. D. 1982. *Principles and practice in second language acquisition*. Oxford: Pergamon.

Morrow, L. M., Pressley, M., Smith, M., and Smith, M. 1997. The effect of a literature-based program integrated into a literacy and science instruction with children from diverse backgrounds. *Reading Research Quarterly* 32 (1): 54–76.

National Council of Teachers of English. 1993. *Elementary school practices: NCTE guidelines and position statements*. [Online]. Available: *www.ncte.org/positions/elem.html*

National Research Council (NRC). 1996. *National science education standards*. Washington, DC: National Academy Press.

Romance, N. R., and Vitale, M. R. 1992. A curriculum strategy that expands time for in-depth elementary science instruction by using science-based reading strategies: Effects of a year-long study in grade four. *Journal of Research in Science Teaching* 29 (6): 545–54.

Ruiz-Primo, M. A., Li, M., and Shavelson, R. 2001. Looking into students' science notebooks: What do teachers do with them? Paper presented at the American Educational Research Association Annual Meeting, 10-14 April, Seattle.

Scarnati, J., and Weller, C. 1992. The write stuff: Science inquiry skills help students think positively about writing assignments. *Science and Children* 29 (4): 28–29.

Shymansky, J. A., Marberry, C. A., and Jorgensen, M. A. 1977. Science and mathematics are spoken and written here. In D. Holdzkom and P. B. Lut, eds., *Reform in math and science education: Issues for the classroom.* Columbus, OH: Eisenhower National Clearinghouse.

Stotsky, S. 1984. Imagination, writing, and the integration of knowledge in the middle grades. *Journal of Teaching Writing* 3 (2): 157–90.

Trueba, H. T., Guthrie, G., and Au, K., eds. 1981. *Culture and the bilingual classroom: Studies in classroom ethnography.* Rowley, MA: Newbury House.

Reaching the Zone of Optimal Learning: The Alignment of Curriculum, Instruction, and Assessment

Stephen J. Farenga, Beverly A. Joyce, and Daniel Ness

Stephen J. Farenga is an associate professor of science education at Dowling College in Oakdale, New York. His research has appeared in a number of major journals in science education, technology, and education of the gifted, and he is a consultant to urban and suburban school districts. He has taught science for fifteen years in both public and private settings at the elementary and secondary levels, has served on the Commissioner's Advisory Council on the Arts in Education in New York State, and is a contributing co-editor to "After the Bell" in *Science Scope.*

Beverly A. Joyce is an associate professor of research, measurement, and evaluation at Dowling College in Oakdale, New York. Beverly's research has appeared in a number of major journals in science education, technology, and education of the gifted. She has taught at public and private colleges in mathematics, psychology, and education departments and has served on advisory committees for the New York and New England offices of the College Board. She is a contributing co-editor to "After the Bell" in *Science Scope.*

Daniel Ness is an assistant professor in mathematics education at Dowling College in Oakdale, New York. He writes extensively in the areas of assessment in mathematics, young children's cognitive abilities in spatial and geometric concepts, the articulation between everyday and in-school mathematical concepts, and the relationship between mathematical thinking and learning science. He is a contributing co-editor to "After the Bell" in *Science Scope.*

Characterizing assessments in terms of components of competence and the content and process demands of the subject matter brings specificity to assessment objectives, such as "higher level thinking" and "deep understanding." This approach links specific content with the underlying cognitive processes and the performance objectives that the teacher has in mind. (Bransford, Brown, and Cocking 2000, 244–45)

This quote challenges traditional thinking about the integration of curriculum, instruction, and assessment. It brings to the forefront the need to examine the relationship of the simultaneous development of curriculum, instruction, assessment, and science learning. How we assess student ability in science content depends on what we define as "components of competence" for achieving "higher level thinking" and "deep understanding." In identifying science content, cognitive processes, and performance objectives, one realizes that curriculum, instruction, and assessment are three components in the learning equation for science literacy.

In this chapter, we discuss the three components and how their integration will help our students achieve a strong knowledge base in science. We begin with a discussion on the conventional thinking regarding the components. After examining more contemporary views, we show how various overlaps of any two components affect scientific learning and literacy. Finally, we demonstrate how the overlap of all three components leads to what we refer to as the Zone of Optimal Learning.

Conventional Thinking about Science Curriculum, Instruction, and Assessment

Studies in curriculum, instruction, and assessment point to a dichotomy between theory and practice. Tyler's (1949) approach to curriculum inquiry attempts to bridge the divide between the development and the delivery of curriculum, instruction, and assessment by advising educators to ask the following questions:

◆ What educational purposes should the school seek to attain?

◆ What educational experiences can be provided that are likely to attain these purposes?

◆ How can these educational experiences be effectively organized?

◆ How can we determine whether these purposes are being attained?

Curriculum, instruction, and assessment have historically been considered three separate entities. Curriculum materials and assessment instruments have been produced by commercial enterprises, state policymakers, university faculty, national professional organizations, and local educational practitioners. Instruction is the one component of the learning formula that is relegated to professional development companies, consultants, higher education faculty, and teachers, but is executed solely by the science teacher.

The literature is replete with studies that examine the effectiveness of reform in each of the three learning components. The reform efforts generally involved the manipulation of some factor of curriculum, instruction, and assessment to maximize students' achievement. Although the studies demonstrate some short-lived gains, large-scale replication did not occur. The failure of sustained achievement in science has led to systemic reform that integrates *simultaneous* change in curriculum, instruction, and assessment. We will examine how each of these components was viewed in the past as a preface to discussing contemporary changes.

Curriculum

Curriculum is the manner in which content is defined, arranged, and emphasized. Serving as the medium in which the teacher interacts with students, curriculum includes structure, organization, and delivery of content. Traditionally, the foundations of curriculum design have been considered as a set of educational activities that are organized and evaluated in a parallel manner (Tyler 1949). Additional elements of curriculum development included students' past and present interests, developmental levels, social outcomes, uses of technology, integration of subject matter, and national and local standards. Curriculum writers stressed the commonality among the sciences such as the reliance on evidence, investigation, and arrangement of factual knowledge into concepts, theories, and principles. The prevalence of these themes is evident in a number of curriculum programs that emanated from the post-Sputnik era. Programs such as the Science Curriculum Improvement Study (SCIS), Science—A Process Approach (SAPA), and the Elementary Science Study (ESS) shared a common thread in fostering hands-on activities, problem-solving skills, and science attitude development, and were seminal in beginning to integrate curriculum, instruction, and assessment. (A more complete list of programs appears in Figure 1.)

Figure 1. Examples of Science Education Programs

AIMS	Activities for Integrating Mathematics and Science
BSCS	Biological Science Curriculum Study
GEMS	Great Explorations in Mathematics and Science
FOSS	Full Option Science System
HumBio	Human Biology Middle Grades' Curriculum Project
OBIS	Outdoor Biology Instructional Program
STC	Science Technology for Children
SAPA	Science-A-Process Approach
SCIS	Science Curriculum Improvement Study
IPS	Introductory Physical Science
ESS	Elementary Science Study

Science curriculum developers also were responsive to the needs of learners in that they articulated the cognitive foundations of science learning. Learning theorists such as Piaget, Ausubel, Gagné, and Bruner recognized that learning is affected by the patterns formed through the integration of what students think and perceive. Science curricula were influenced by Piaget's stage theory, Ausubel's use of advanced organizers, Gagné's learning hierarchy, and Bruner's discovery learning. Each learning theorist added to the field of constructivism by recognizing that new experiences are contextualized by prior knowledge.

Instruction

Instruction is the conduit through which teachers provide or facilitate factual, conceptual, or procedural knowledge to their students. The interpretation of curriculum has required teachers to develop instructional plans around goals or purposes. The proliferation of science programs during the post-Sputnik era led to changes in instruction that are still prevalent. Piaget's theory of learning, for example, illustrated a three-phase learning cycle, which is made up of an exploratory hands-on phase, a concept development phase, and a concept application phase (Atkin and Karplus 1962). It is remarkable to consider that this theory of instruction, developed in the early 1960s, has been translated into a cutting-edge form of educational practice today. During the exploration phase, students ask questions about their understanding of phenomena while engaged in mental and physical activity. In this phase, students gather data based on their observations and the teacher is the facilitator, asking questions and stimulating thought. During the concept development phase, the teacher promotes new ideas based on student observations. Here, the teacher fosters the recognition of patterns in data to reveal concepts under study. Instruction during this stage may take numerous forms, including lecture and textbook readings, to promote conceptual gain. The final instructional phase—concept application—requires students to extend or transfer their understanding of a concept to a new situation. During this stage, students' misunderstandings are identified and corrected.

Traditionally, elements of instruction have included the selection of method and material, and classroom organization and management. Formulated instructional procedures allowed teachers to pursue their objectives while using various pedagogies. Instruction was considered effective when the intended learning outcomes were achieved as reflected through observable behavior.

Assessment

Valid assessment provides samples of behavior that allow the classroom teacher to observe and evaluate student responses indicating conceptual knowledge or understanding of a scientific topic. These samples of behavior—or observable student responses—are elicited through informal teacher queries during a science laboratory experiment or formal, comprehensive examinations at the end of the semester. The content area and level of behavioral objectives of the assessment techniques have ranged from mastering fundamental building blocks to integrating concepts at a higher level. The critical evidence of valid assessment is the appropriate match between what has been taught and what is being tested. Standardized tests (e.g., national, regional, and statewide) have played a major role in science education assessment; however, traditional and alternative forms of classroom-initiated formats (e.g., journals, group evaluations, teacher observations, well-focused classroom tests, and performance assessments) have also emerged as valuable tools in a comprehensive assessment program.

Many new forms of science curricula and instruction that were developed during the 1960s supported broad reforms in assessment. Program objectives required students to demonstrate what they learned using authentic activities. These new activities paralleled situations found outside the classroom and mirrored scientific endeavors. Students were required to integrate procedural ("how to do it") knowledge and declarative ("what they know") knowledge. Programs such as SCIS, SAPA, and ESS opened the door to more valid and realistic measures of student understanding. These programs recognized the importance of aligning curriculum, instruction, and assessment to reach the Zone of Optimal Learning.

Contemporary Views of Curriculum, Instruction, and Assessment

During the past decade, specific changes in science curriculum, instruction, and assessment have unfolded as a result of learning standards in science education. Whereas past efforts in reform grossly undervalued classroom teachers in regard to the design of curriculum, instruction, and assessment, current reform agents are cognizant that successful changes take place at a grassroots level. National reform movements promoted by the American Association for the Advancement of Science, for example, recognize this need and include teachers as contributors to reform projects (e.g., Project 2061: Science For All Americans [1990] and Project 2061: Benchmarks for Science Literacy [1993]).

The current reform movement has changed the manner in which curriculum, instruction, and assessment are developed and implemented. These changes have given the educational community insight into "best practices" in science teaching and learning. Through clinical observation of teachers, we have developed a composite of best practices as demonstrated in the scenario of Ms. Reeves (Figure 2). Teachers can use the scenario to examine their own practices by asking the following questions:

◆ Is Ms. Reeves following any particular guidelines that are influencing the material she is delivering to her students?

◆ Does Ms. Reeves appear to be following or varying any particular instructional pedagogies?

◆ Does Ms. Reeves utilize any particular procedures for assessing her students' abilities in science?

Figure 2. Scenario: Ms. Reeves's Classroom

Clinical Classroom Analysis

Ms. Reeves teaches an eighth-grade physical science lesson following the district's curriculum guidelines. She wanted her students to discover the relationship between heat absorption and color. She posed the question: "How does the color of the material affect its ability to absorb energy?" Some students believed that color made no difference, while others thought that there was a correlation between color and absorption of heat. Ms. Reeves then asked students what materials they might need to conduct the experiment. Together, they decided on the materials and how to use them. She divided the class into teams of four, and reviewed safety procedures for handling glassware and hot objects. Each team received five cans: black, yellow, white, red, and silver. Ms. Reeves had the students fill the cans with potting soil. Each team received five thermometers which they inserted in the soil at a depth of 4 cm. The cans were then placed under a 200-watt lamp with reflector, equidistant from the heat source. The students agreed to read the thermometers every 30 seconds for 20 minutes and record their data readings in a chart. Next, students used the data to construct a graph.

Ms. Reeves facilitates science lessons in a number of ways. Her lessons are generally student-centered and inquiry-based. Students' background knowledge is informally assessed through observation and conversation. Ms. Reeves identifies students' misconceptions, and designs activities to promote basic understanding. She accomplishes this task through various pedagogical methods, from direct instruction to open-ended inquiry. As students work in teams,

Ms. Reeves facilitates learning by watching and listening to them as they make decisions. Understanding the importance of discussing ideas and making conjectures, Ms. Reeves encourages her students to explain their problem-solving methods. While students work on problems, Ms. Reeves observes them and asks about the ways they are figuring out solutions. While walking around the room, Ms. Reeves develops anecdotal records on what she observes and of her students' responses regarding methods of problem solving. Some of her questions to students are: Which can had the greatest temperature change? How do you know that this solution is correct? How does the color of the material affect its ability to absorb energy? How did you determine the solution? What problems did you incur while completing the activity?

Zone of Optimal Learning

Our theory-based, clinically applied model (see Figure 3) summons Tyler's rationale for approaches to curriculum inquiry and its discussion of parallel construction of curriculum, instruction, and assessment. The Zone of Optimal Learning represents a best-fit model of the integration of these three components. It is at this juncture that they are optimally aligned. In the Zone of Optimal Learning, students are afforded the opportunity to display "components of competence" for achieving "higher level thinking" and "deep understanding." However, partial alignments of the three components create integrated learning domains—Curriculum-Instruction, Instruction-Assessment, or Curriculum-Assessment—which create partial learning opportunities. We discuss each domain below, focusing on the missing component in each case in order to identify what the science teacher can do to move his or her students toward the Zone of Optimal Learning.

Figure 3. Theory-based, Clinically Applied Model: A Strategy for Aligning Curriculum, Instruction, and Assessment

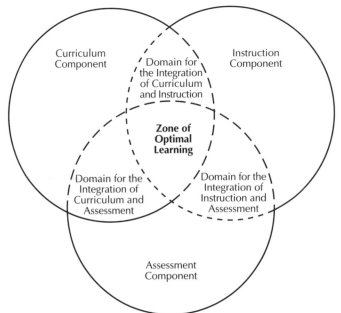

Curriculum-Instruction

At this domain of integration, only curriculum and instruction are aligned. However, science teachers and their students rely on assessment data—or test results—to evaluate how well the instructional content has been mastered. Throughout the year, teachers collect data to reinforce student learning and modify instruction. The need for feedback is generally better served by formative classroom assessment—both in terms of timeliness and specificity—than by summative assessment (for the differences, see Figure 4). This is evidenced by Ms. Reeves's use of structured analysis, contextual observation, and tacit dialogue (Ness, in press). As illustrated in the scenario, Ms. Reeves encourages her students to conjecture and reason through their problems as they are engaged in scientific inquiry. This is an example of structured analysis—a method of assessment that allows the teacher to evaluate students as they share their own strategies of solving problems. Ms. Reeves also walks around the room taking anecdotal notes of her observations of students engaged in problem-solving activities. This assessment procedure—contextual observation—is an activity-based observational technique that captures samples of behavior of each student.

In addition, as shown at the end of the scenario, Ms. Reeves queries each student as a means of detecting his or her constructed knowledge. This form of direct questioning demonstrates Ms. Reeves's use of tacit dialogue—moments of verbal exchange between teacher and student whereby the teacher extracts information about or understanding of the individual student through additional samples of behavior. The structured analysis, contextual observation, and tacit dialogue techniques provide formative feedback, and make visible students' understanding to both the teacher and peers. As evidenced by the informal exchanges between Ms. Reeves and her students, Bloom's (1980, 24) assertion that "formative testing...may be considered as examples of cybernetic feedback—corrective procedures necessary for almost all human activities" still rings true.

Figure 4. Examples of Formative and Summative Assessment Tools

Formative Assessment Tools—Data collection tools used during the teaching and learning process to modify instruction to promote higher-level thinking and deep understanding.

Teacher-Initiated Interaction
- Structured analysis
- Contextual observation
- Tacit dialogue

Informal Evaluation
- Checklists
- Quizzes
- Self and peer evaluation

Summative Assessment Tools—Assessment tools used to assign grades, make placement decisions, and certify achievement.

Final Evaluation Tools
- Multiple-choice/short answer tests
- Essay tests
- Journals
- Research reports
- Portfolios

Performance Tools
- Laboratory demonstrations
- Presentations
- Process skills tests

Instruction-Assessment

At this juncture, curriculum is not aligned with instruction and assessment. Textbook publishers have been responsible for defining the unofficial national curriculum and failing to make this alignment. Textbooks are intentionally designed to include content topics and process skills that cover the lowest common denominator among all schools. Recognizing this problem, the AAAS's Project 2061 developed *Benchmarks for Science Literacy* (1993), which gives educators a blueprint to use in fashioning local curricula. The Benchmarks—which identify thresholds of performance, a common core of knowledge, and specific goals in science literacy—have empowered states, professional associations, community agencies, and teachers to design curriculum to meet local demands. This shift in control allows teachers to move from being interpreters of curriculum prescribed by program designers to being curriculum architects. The result is congruence between the curriculum plan and what is taught in the classroom.

Ms. Reeves recognizes the importance of playing an active role in designing curriculum, defining instructional objectives, and developing valid assessment tools to ensure maximum overlap. By contributing to district curriculum plans, she is moving her classroom closer to the Zone of Optimal Learning.

Curriculum-Assessment

This partial overlap occurs when state or federal agencies develop a course of study and method of assessment. It is prevalent with large-scale science curriculum projects that mandate specific content, scripted lessons, and prescribed assessment. Aligning curriculum and assessment at the expense of instruction, however, ignores a critical component of the model. The teacher generally has limited latitude to turn the curriculum into lessons and activities that are appropriate for his or her students, who may vary by economic status, ethnicity, community standards, and academic status. Because instruction serves as the medium for delivering content, students' knowledge base depends almost exclusively on how teachers express content, and not on curriculum development or assessment practices. Differentiated instruction is hampered because it is reliant upon the teacher's ability to interpret the curriculum and assessment. Matching the content of both the curriculum and assessment exclusively (e.g., statewide curriculum and examinations) suggests little or no teacher involvement. Teacher instruction may be reduced to merely "teaching to the test."

Working toward a Zone of Optimal Learning: Teachers on the Front Line

The empowerment of the classroom teacher results in the substantive linking of the established curriculum, instructional objectives, and methods of assessment. When that link has been made, the teacher's pedagogical repertoire will blend direct instruction and inquiry-learning strategies to foster the construction of knowledge. Constructivist philosophy recognizes that knowledge is accumulated from a wide array of teaching methods (Bransford, Brown, and Cocking 2000). Each student enters school with a unique background of experiences and understanding, and so teachers must recognize a student's strengths (in terms of science content) and the manner in which he or she learns best (in terms of instructional method). Methods may range from lecture to activity-based instruction. Irrespective of how one is taught, one still constructs knowledge.

The essence of *direct instruction* is to help the student acquire broad factual knowledge to enhance basic cognitive and communication process skills. This method of instruction is useful in filling students' knowledge gaps that may hinder inquiry-based science instruction. With direct instruction, the locus of control rests with the teacher, whose function is to monitor and direct students' classroom concentration and persistence. Direct instruction necessitates that the curriculum be carefully sequenced throughout the instructional process.

Open-ended inquiry is less structured than direct teaching and places the locus of control on the student. The process of inquiry requires students to start with a question, design an investigation, develop a hypothesis, collect data, use data to answer the original question, determine whether the original question requires modification, and communicate results. Studies in cognitive science suggest that one must have a knowledge base in order to pose appropriate questions, easily assimilate additional knowledge, and effectively judge the correctness of information (Landauer and Dumais 1996; Larkin et al. 1980; Miller and Gildea 1987). The true inquiry process is open-ended, generally leading to additional questions. The process seems linear; however, the skills necessary to proceed through the investigation have varying levels of difficulty. It is evident that students are not at the same starting point in terms of prior knowledge, abilities, and interests. To maximize the benefit of inquiry, the teacher tailors the activity to accommodate the students' experiential profiles (Farenga and Joyce 1997). This tailoring process produces a new strain of inquiry that integrates techniques from direct instruction and open-ended inquiry—that is, "adaptive inquiry."

Direct instruction and open-ended inquiry are both effective strategies for teaching science. However, when used exclusively, each strategy ignores individual differences and leaves instructional gaps. Teachers need to select curriculum, assess prior knowledge, and design the delivery of instruction to match the cognitive level of the student. As instruction is delivered, the teacher must assess student responses and move the student from concrete understanding to more abstract conceptual development. Simultaneous processing of information is obtained from the delivery of instruction, students' outcomes, and prior knowledge. This continuous feedback and interpretation of information related to content, instruction, and assessment are the basis of *adaptive inquiry*.

Adaptive inquiry is the product of the synergistic relationship between what a student brings to the classroom and the teacher's ability to shape a lesson in response to the needs of the student. The process of designing inquiry-based lessons is primarily influenced by students' prior knowledge, the curriculum, and method of assessment. Flexibility in the design, assessment, and communication of results is paramount to foster the concept of science as inquiry at work. By implementing a focus and review strategy in a lesson, the teacher is able to assess students' prior knowledge and understanding of the topic. Ms. Reeves demonstrates this proficiency by identifying students' misconceptions, and designs activities to promote basic understanding.

Observations of Today's Classroom

Our extensive observations suggest that the pressures on teachers in today's classrooms to maximize student achievement demand the realignment of curriculum, instruction, and assessment. Clearly, the roles of teachers and students have been redefined. The teacher, no longer the single source of information, assumes the active role of facilitator. Students, who passively accepted knowledge from the teacher, are now responsible for collecting data, evaluating information, explaining results, and constructing their own knowledge base. To measure the degree of knowledge gained by students, these shifts require modifications in assessment techniques. The augmentation of alternative assessment techniques with traditional testing provides a program that studies the final products and the thinking processes that contributed to them. Excluding either element—alternative or traditional assessment—will ignore a major source of data regarding students' achievement and understanding. An appropriate balance between the two forms of assessment must be established by the classroom teacher based on the composition of her classroom, the purpose of the assessment, and the content or objectives to be covered. The same issues of validity apply to both designing an assessment program and constructing a single test.

With an arsenal of traditional and alternative techniques, teachers can match the assessment tool with the purpose of assessment. We have found that teachers often use a traditional test to evaluate students' baseline knowledge and then proceed to a performance-based activity. On other occasions, we have noticed that teachers who begin their lessons with a performance assessment do so with the aim of piquing students' interest in various science topics. Steps for implementing performance assessment techniques include the following:

◆ Develop an appropriate performance task list (in the form of a rubric).

◆ Identify the content, product, or processes to be assessed.

◆ Display a model; discuss its features and how it relates to the performance task list.

◆ Engage students in the activity using the performance task list as a scaffold to master the skills required by the task.

◆ Have students evaluate their products or processes in terms of the performance task list.

◆ Use the performance task list to evaluate students' performance.

◆ Have students discuss the evaluation of their performance.

Regardless of technique, rather than construing assessment as a gauge by which students are rated and compared in order of competence, teachers need to think of assessment as providing students with formative feedback (as suggested by Bloom's notion of cybernetic feedback) on individual products or elements of performance. Moreover, assessment should allow students to determine their own benchmarks for improvement; the aim of these benchmarks is to provide students with useful information for tapping their own strengths.

Conclusion

The integrity of the curriculum, instruction, and assessment structure is based on substantive links among the established curriculum, instructional objectives, and methods of assessment. Careful scrutiny of these three elements confirms the interconnection of curriculum goals, instructional intent, and assessment validity.

The dynamic process of integrating these elements is the first step in meeting the challenge of increasing science literacy. Applying the curriculum, instruction, and assessment model is a field-based experiment that requires the teacher to think and act like a scientist. As with any other experiment, he or she must identify the research problem, define the variables to be manipulated, run trials, and make data-driven decisions based on the results. This experimental approach will assist teacher-scientists to move their classrooms into the Zone of Optimal Learning.

References

American Association for the Advancement of Science (AAAS). 1990. *Science for all Americans*. New York: Oxford University Press.

———. 1993. *Benchmarks for science literacy*. New York: Oxford University Press.

Atkin, J. M., and Karplus, R. 1962. Discovery or invention? *The Science Teacher* 29 (5): 45.

Bloom, B. S. 1980. The new direction in educational research: Alterable variables. In W. S. Schrader, ed., *Measuring achievement: Progress of a decade, new directions for testing and measurement,* 17–30. San Francisco: Jossey-Bass.

Bransford, J. D., Brown, A. L., and Cocking, R. R., eds. 2000. *How people learn: Brain, mind, experience, and school*. Washington, DC: National Academy Press.

Farenga, S. J., and. Joyce, B.A. 1997. What children bring to the classroom: Learning science from experience. *School Science and Mathematics* 97 (5): 248–52.

Farenga, S. J., and Joyce, B. A. In press. Teaching youngsters science in a culturally diverse inner-city classroom. In A. C. Diver-Stamnes and L. A. Catelli, eds., *Commitment to excellence: Transforming teaching and teacher education in inner-city and urban settings*. Englewood Cliffs, NJ: Hampton Press.

Landauer, T., and Dumais, S. 1996. *How come you know so much? From practical problems to new memory theory*. In D. J. Hermann, C. McEvoy, C. Hertzog, P. Hertel, and M. K. Johnson, eds., *Basic and applied memory research, vol. 1*. Mahwah, NJ: Lawrence Erlbaum.

Larkin, J., McDermott, J., Simon, D. P., and. Simon, H. A. 1980. Expert and novice performance in solving physics problems. *Science* 208: 1335–42.

Miller, G. A., and Gildea, P. 1987. How children learn words. *Scientific American* (Sept.): 94–99.

Ness, D. In press. Helping teachers recognize and connect the culturally-bound nature of young children's mathematical intuitions to in-school mathematics concepts. In A. C. Diver-Stamnes and L. A. Catelli, eds., *Commitment to excellence: Transforming teaching and teacher education in inner-city and urban settings.* Englewood Cliffs, NJ: Hampton Press.

Tyler, R. W. 1949. *Basic principles of curriculum and instruction.* Chicago: University of Chicago Press.

National Science Teachers Association

PART 3

Teaching That Enhances Student Learning

Alignment of Instruction with Knowledge of Student Learning

Paul Jablon

Paul Jablon is director of science for the Everett Public Schools in Everett, Massachusetts, a small city on the outskirts of Boston. After eleven years as a professor of science education, first as program head at Brooklyn College, City University of New York, and then in the Graduate School of Education at the University of Massachusetts-Lowell, he decided to return to public schools where he is applying the best of what we know about how students learn to his own classroom teaching and to systemic change within the district. Over three decades he has directed nationally recognized urban school change projects that have had a direct impact on the way thousands of teachers approach science teaching and learning. He has received numerous awards from the Science Council of New York and the New York Biology Teachers Association for outstanding service, teaching, and lifetime achievement. He is best known for having created and co-directed the BONGO Program, one of the most effective and well-documented programs for urban at-risk adolescents.

The emphasis on establishing communities of scientific practice builds on the fact that robust knowledge and understandings are socially constructed through talk, activity, and interaction around meaningful problems and tools. The teacher guides and supports students as they explore problems and define questions that are of interest to them. A community of practice also provides direct cognitive and social support for the efforts of the group's individual members. Students share the responsibility for thinking and doing: they distribute their intellectual activity so that the burden for managing the whole process does not fall to any one individual. In addition, a community of practice can be a powerful context for constructing scientific meanings. In challenging one another's thoughts and beliefs, students must be explicit about their meanings; they must negotiate conflicts in belief or evidence; they must share and synthesize their knowledge to achieve understanding.
(Bransford, Brown, and Cocking 1999, 172)

Teachers and school science departments have been trying for the past two decades to adapt their teaching practices to align with the emerging knowledge of how humans learn. Significant advances have been made on a *procedural* level. The surface structure of many classrooms has changed, appearing more student-centered, with students sitting in groups and engaged in hands-on activity. However, because deeper *cultural* issues have rarely been addressed, the impact of the *procedural* changes has been constrained. The underlying interactions and goals have for the most part remained unaltered (Tobin 1990; Flick et al. 1997). The gradual *proce-*

dural changes in teaching have not created classroom communities that reflect the scope of ideas for science classroom practice delineated in the above quotation and have not significantly affected science achievement.

A small number of teachers and departments have, however, radically altered the *culture* of their classrooms to reflect these new understandings and found the effectiveness of the changes startling both in the cognitive and affective performance of their students (White and Frederickson 1997, 1998). Both the students' and the teachers' roles have shifted: the types of expectations, social interactions, level of cognitive application, methods of communicating understanding, and acceptance of responsibility for assessing learning have all been redistributed to better match our understandings of how our brain remembers, understands, reasons, and transfers skills. Consider the following scenario concerning ninth-grade students in one of our urban schools. Please realize that these teachers' classrooms and their students are composites of actual classrooms and students that have been observed and interviewed.

Scenario #1—The Classroom

Let's look in on the science class of Marie, a student in an urban high school.

It was a surprisingly warm spring day. Marie's science class had started off with a bang—actually more like a crumple, as her teacher had made a large gallon metal can crinkle up by heating and cooling it. The demonstration had drawn Marie's attention, but the teacher's background instruction since then about air pressure and temperature had become increasingly less engaging. She took the opportunity to get a hall pass for the bathroom as he began to write some equation with Ps and Ts on the board. She didn't want to be around as she rarely had the right answer when he called on her about equations. Maybe the teacher would be finished by the time she got back and they would start a lab. Not that labs were the greatest things, but at least she got to handle some stuff and have her teacher explain something directly to her. She wondered, though, why, even though her teacher could always explain things so clearly, she could just not remember how to do the problems once she got home.

As she walked down the hallway toward the restroom, she heard a familiar laugh come from Mrs. Thomas's classroom. She immediately recognized it as her friend Patti's giggle. She stopped to look into the classroom. Students were grouped in twos and fours and seemed to be playing with some extra-large syringes with short pieces of plastic fish-tank tubing attached to the tip instead of a needle. She watched as her friend pushed the plunger down while holding her finger tightly over the end of the tube. "See," Patti exclaimed to the three other students in her group, "the tip of the plunger always comes back to the same place." One of the other students immediately responded, "the exact same place?" To which Patti responded, "Yeah, well eventually…. Well, I think it's exactly the same place…. Uh, let's try it again and see. Why don't you hold it this time, Greg?" Similar conversations were going on all about the room. Some seemed more like arguments; others were more casual. Mrs. Thomas "cruised" about the room reminding students to write down some of their findings and ideas. Occasionally she would ask a group or an individual a question about what they were thinking. She warned everyone in the room that someone from each group would be reporting back to the "whole scientific community" in a few minutes so the groups needed to get their thoughts and questions together. The noise and turmoil of the room gradually turned into a contrasting quiet. One by one, reporters from groups began to report back what they thought had occurred when they manipulated the materials. At first Mrs. Thomas had to ask the others in the class if they had any "critical dialogue" for the group reporting. Some started to ask for evidence for the claims made by groups. Others noted that certain phenomenon reported didn't seem to match what they had observed. Soon students were asking questions and making suggestions all on their own. Certain students kept asking everybody why things were happening. People had the hardest times responding to this "why" question.

Within ten minutes Mrs. Thomas had the discussion focused on a number of students' notion that the "air" in the "tube" of the syringe could be "compressed" into a smaller space by pushing down on the "plunger." Mrs. Thomas immediately wrote each idea, and each modification of an idea, on large newsprint papers she had taped on the walls. There seemed to be old piles of written-on newsprint papers all about the classroom as well. She pulled out those papers with students' relevant ideas from past classes, sometimes changing what was written on those old sheets based on new evidence from today's investigation, and rehung them on the wall. She had the students create what she called "operational definitions" of all these words, ideas, and relationships between words and ideas and wrote and modified them in another color marker as people reported. The only thing that everyone in the class could seem to agree upon as they asked questions of one another, in a surprisingly respectful way, was that as the space, which some people were now calling volume, got smaller the pressure got greater, and vice versa. There was lots of confusion about what the "stuff" in the tube was, whether the amount of "stuff" changed as it was pushed into the smaller space: Were we talking about the air "having pressure" or the pressure of our fingers on the plunger, and were force and pressure the same thing, and lots of other related questions. There seemed to be more questions than answers. Just as Mrs. Thomas was writing down all the questions that groups were most interested in on another sheet of paper, the bell rang. At that moment Marie realized she was in deep trouble as she ran back to her own classroom. If she had stayed, she would have heard Mrs. Thomas ask each student to write two things for homework: first, what did they think the relationship between pressure and volume was for air in the syringe and what was their evidence? and second, what question did they most want to find an answer to after manipulating the syringe and listening to the discussion? Many of the students noisily discussed these points as they packed their things and walked into the hallway to their next class.

Some underlying assumptions about learning can be extracted from this scenario, but others are not as obvious from this small classroom "slice of life." During this part of Mrs. Thomas's instruction

◆ She gave no answers to questions if she thought that students could uncover some insight on their own.

◆ She gave no background information prior to the lesson, but allowed students to start by exploring a particular broad physical phenomenon.

◆ The students revealed to her their individual and group preconceptions of this phenomenon as they explained, and defended with evidence, their thinking. She understands that students come to the classroom already knowing something about the phenomenon and that any new, more coherent, and deeper understanding they will create will be a reconstruction of these original ideas through their own struggles with the issues.

◆ She allowed the students to construct their own naive, incipient understanding about and among concepts. This awareness will allow her to anticipate some of her students' confusion and recognize why the students have difficulty grasping particular alternative ideas.

◆ She not only expected, but welcomed, "mistakes" in both concepts and reasoning, which she also expected to be remedied by further work by individuals and groups of students. She expects her students to eventually learn to determine for themselves if they understand.

◆ She expected students and groups to frame some testable questions about the relationship among factors that they thought played a role in this phenomenon.

◆ Students were expected to negotiate ideas with one another.

◆ The classroom modeled the notions of peer review and verification. What the classroom scientific community "knows" is based on students' own observations, discussions, and analysis, and reference to their own prior investigations, knowledge, and reading. Their knowledge is tentative and evolving, with current understandings posted daily on newsprint and in student journals.

Scenario #2—Student Understanding

Some additional insight into Mrs. Thomas's alignment of her practice with her understanding of how people learn can be garnered from a conversation Marie might have had with her friend Patti a few days later during lunch. As with the classroom scenario, this conversation is a scenario created from a composite of extensive interviews with urban students.

"Hi, Patti. I can't believe they're serving hamburgers again. Actually it's more like mystery meat. Speaking of mysteries, I was watching you in Mrs. Thomas's class on Tuesday. That is sure some flipped-out class. Why were you arguing with Greg about that syringe stuff?"

"If you drown it in ketchup, it's not too bad. Yeah, Greg was really on my case about my being so sure that the pressure was going to push the plunger to the same place. He sure can be nitpicking sometimes. On the other hand he is cute."

"Greg, cute? Well, to each his own. Who cares about air pressure anyway? I'm studying the same junk in my class. PV = nrT. Boring. I can never tell which thing to put into which part of the equation."

"Actually, I was arguing because I thought I was right. Eventually, I found a lot of evidence to support my idea. When I wrote up my ideas about that for homework, Mrs. Thomas gave me a 'B so far' and wrote a lot of questions that helped me think it through better."

"How could she give you homework? There were no notes on the board and your class couldn't even agree on anything. And what in the world is a 'B so far'"?

"You're right. We hadn't figured out much yet about the air pressure stuff. But yesterday and today we worked on some more investigations and some of the ideas are starting to get a little clearer. The class has come up with a set of 'physical laws' about pressure and volume we all agree upon so far. Our 'theories' for why it happens are still all over the place. Actually, we argue all the time. It's kind of fun. The teacher says that we are just 'getting a feel for the territory' of this air pressure stuff; just trying to figure out all the stuff that affects it. Just today there were three groups who said that temperature had something to do with both the pressure and volume. They were talking about warm and cold soda bottles. So she sent them off with ice and warm water and the syringes, and they are designing investigations about the effects of temperature. She gave some of us tire pressure gauges, tire pumps, and thermometers to go home tonight and mess around with our bicycle tires before and after riding and after we pumped in air."

"So what's this 'B so far' business?"

"She makes us revise all our assignments. Sometimes she reads them and asks the questions first and other times other students do it first. Then we rethink and rewrite our ideas. Sometimes we need to write only what process we went through in figuring out our answers. Sometimes we just need to write good questions. She calls it 'meta-something or other.' She says we need to pay attention to how we figure stuff out—how we plan, how we try to connect ideas."

"You mean you can always get a better grade by redoing it? That's cool."

"Well, you don't want to be really redoing the whole thing. You can never keep up then. That's why I'm always glad to be able to try my thinking out in front of the class when I can't quite figure stuff out. It makes writing about my thinking easier."

"Don't you feel dumb in front of the class when you don't know the right answer?"

"I used to feel embarrassed, but not as much any more. Actually it helps me understand better. She's more concerned with us thinking about our thinking and building a better set of ways of approaching problems to get answers."

"But you were so adamant with Greg about that air pressure junk. Can I have those French fries if you are not going to finish them?"

"Here, but they're soggy. Well actually, I became a little interested in it when we were using the air quality monitor. This unit we're doing is about some report we need to make to the school board about the quality of air in the various parts of the school. This whole issue of air pressure came up when we were trying to figure out how to get our air samples in the bags into the monitor ports. Do you know that we were getting high carbon monoxide readings in some classrooms? Anthony thinks that one of the air intake vents for our school is right by the loading dock."

"Yeah, so what's the big deal? Why doesn't Mrs. Thomas just tell you if this is a problem or not? Doesn't she ever tell you anything? I couldn't ever pass those Friday tests if my teacher didn't write notes on the board. That textbook is Greek to me."

"Can I have that ketchup? Thanks. After we investigate something for a long time and we have exhausted ourselves coming up with evidence to support our 'laws' and 'theories,' then she let's us in on what the rest of the scientists in the world have learned. She relates it back to some big idea like systems or balance so we can see it's just another example of that big idea and not something completely new. By then I can actually follow what she is talking about because I know so much about the topic from our own work. Also, since we design and redesign so many investigations I can actually follow the famous experiments when I read about them in the science text."

"Patti! You are really weirding me out! You actually sound like you like this science nonsense."

"Hey. I'm not saying it's my favorite subject, but it does grow on you. It's way better than listening to the teacher talk. I actually get to do stuff. And I really feel good when she makes us apply something we learned to a completely different topic and I can figure the new stuff out. Or at least I can get close to figuring it out. That really makes me feel cool. And when I can't figure it out she has a place in the lab report to write about your frustrations."

Now it becomes much clearer that Mrs. Thomas has synthesized much of our understanding about how the brain operates and how people learn, and she has incorporated this understanding into her classroom practice. For example:

◆ Since our short-term memory can hold only a limited number of ideas that we need to process in order to make meaning by comparing new insights to our old understandings, she allows students' new conceptions to be richer than their recent observations and analysis by "chunking" these into larger concepts that arise all term long. In this case the gas laws fell into the more general and synthesizing categories of systems and balance. These "chunks" contain previously synthesized concepts that allow the students a broader understanding of this otherwise isolated phenomenon. They notice features and meaningful patterns of information and see underlying principles. (Simon 1980)

◆ She starts with everyday student talk, and eventually she and the students extract from this the relevant scientific concepts and skills; she slowly introduces vocabulary after concepts are understood (progressive formalization).

◆ She expects the students to be metacognitive about their science learning. She assists them in doing this by having students constantly explain their thinking to one another and to her about both procedural knowledge (the processes) and declarative knowledge (the science concepts that they are formulating). She strives to make students' thinking visible. The class spends a majority of the week designing and carrying out real physical investigations in order to construct their understandings and to build their reasoning skills. She knows that if students truly understand how they create knowledge in science, then they can acquire habits of mind that allow them to care about using this process in their daily lives. The propensities to seek evidence, be curious, desire accuracy and precision, and ask for a "fair test" by controlling variables literally becomes part of the fabric of their thinking; it becomes a natural, organic neurological pattern that they apply intuitively in the appropriate places.

◆ She knows her students will be likely to apply both their declarative and procedural knowledge in the appropriate context—that is, to transfer the knowledge in
applicable situations—because she gives them numerous opportunities to apply
the concepts and skills as they are acquiring them to new situations. One group of
students was already off on their own applying some of their evolving insights
about pressure and volume by designing some investigations about the third inter-
vening variable of temperature. Others were applying these naive understandings
to everyday occurrences such as bicycle tires. All of this work is going to have a
larger social importance when the procedural and declarative knowledge are applied to the air quality studies they are doing and publicly reporting. It will truly
intersect with their larger community. In each of these variations, contrasted cases
need to be analyzed so that the concepts become clearer. This process is an example of the Learning Cycle (the exploration, concept introduction, and application phases), STS-based education (Science, Technology, and Society relationships), and classroom inquiry being used seamlessly (Lawson 1995). Although
Mrs. Thomas has started with a complex, project- and community-based task,
through the students' smaller investigations and her large concept referents the
world becomes less complex and more predictable.

◆ She also creates a model of the scientific enterprise in her own room as students
experience personally the creation and ongoing revision of the class's laws and
theories over a period of weeks and months. She is also overt about how this is the
same and different from how the larger scientific enterprise in the world works. In
both this understanding and the previous one, she sees that learning is promoted
by social norms that value the search for understanding.

◆ She understands that teachers can learn more from the questions that the students
frame than from their answers.

◆ The students' lab reports use the left side of the page for the "objective," cognitive
reasoning description of each student's involvement in the investigation and sense-
making about it. The right side of each page is the "affective" side, where the student writes not only about how she or he feels while doing the investigation but also
about the interaction of her or his research team and how all this intersects with the
rest of the student's life. Students use the various brain systems connected to each of
these types of thinking as they do science. (Squire and Kandel 2000)

Additional Classroom Scaffolding

What is not seen in either of these scenarios is another set of scaffolding experiences
that Mrs. Thomas provides her students so that they can intellectually and socially
engage in the way described.

◆ Sometime during each week she includes a brief conflict resolution, responsive
classroom, or cooperative learning activity so that students can learn to respect-

fully listen, interact, disagree, and resolve conflicts, mostly on their own. For example, the activity might demonstrate how to set up a win-win situation versus a win-lose or a lose-lose situation or how to show someone that you are listening and processing what he or she is saying.

◆ The students' questions and investigations grow out of real world projects or previous physical investigations they have created, unlike most science classrooms where we as science teachers answer all the questions that the students don't have.

◆ Effective use of wait-time after open-ended questions, critical dialogue, and active investigations require larger blocks than typically available. Mrs. Thomas's school still uses 55-minute periods; however, she has worked with the principal so that she and her colleagues take these five periods and redistribute them during the week into two double periods and a single period.

◆ She helps students organize their work schedule for the course relative to the rest of their school and social lives by supplying each of them with a mimeographed calendar planning book. Each week they go over benchmarks and mechanisms for getting to those benchmarks. She requests that they write their social engagements and other subject area assignments in this same book. This eventually leads to apportioning time and planning-ahead strategies that become self-regulatory habits of mind. (Bereiter and Scardamalia 1989)

◆ Although she has worked long and hard to develop some specific strategies for her second language learners and special education students (e.g., whom she groups them with), she understands that the science learning strategies she employs for everyone in her class mirror some of the most effective strategies for both these groups.

◆ She is in constant cognitive and affective dialogue with her students, both in class and in her extensive written responses to their written work. Students are constantly revising their work; reconstructing their understanding; literally altering the functional organization of their brains. She understands that by doing so they create the coherent structures of information in their brains that underly effective comprehension and thinking. (Beaulieu and Cynader 1990)

◆ And finally, she has a deep understanding of a way to organize her class throughout the year so that the science concepts, small classroom investigations, larger public projects, process and problem-solving skills, and topics of interest to students are best structured to reach her intended goals. Table 1 delineates how she designs her school year, optimally using each of these organizing elements.

Table 1. The Use of Organizing Elements to Structure Classroom Practice

Organizers for Students	Sub-Organizers for Students
From the students' perspective, the school term is organized around one or two large projects that are active investigations of a real problem in the community. Learners are more motivated when they can use their knowledge to have an impact on others.	Embedded in each of these large projects are a number of smaller investigations of scientific phenomena or simulations of science, technology, and society (STS) interactions. Their order of arrival evolves naturally as students confront the need for understanding the science and STS relationships in order to complete their projects. This process is inherently different from the normal order of "science topics" that derive from a scope and sequence.
Organizers for Teachers	**Overarching Conceptual Organizers for Teachers**
Using the *National Science Education Standards* (NRC 1996) as a reference, the teacher identifies a number of developmentally appropriate conceptual understandings, science process and problem-solving skills, and scientific habits of mind that the students will construct or cultivate by engaging in meaning-making while involved in the project and investigations. These appear in many of the investigations and are revisited so that they are transferable to various contexts (conditionalized).	Overarching conceptual organizers make the world more predictable and scientific conceptual explanations of phenomena more generalizable. For each of the science disciplines, there are four to six concepts to which all other subconcepts can be attached. As the students uncover underlying concepts while they investigate various phenomena, the teacher consistently points out how this more particular interaction is just another example of one of these referents (e.g., conservation of mass and energy, entropy, orogeny, homeostasis, particle and wave nature of matter and energy). In addition to these, there are even broader concepts that the scientific world uses to explain nature—systems, energy, and balance, to name a few.

Mrs. Thompson did not develop her way of teaching without external curriculum resources. She is building on structured, inquiry-based curricula that take into account current knowledge about how students build conceptual understanding and link important ideas. The art of teaching is to use such knowledge as a foundation while responding creatively to the nuances of the thinking of real students. Her colleagues have been gradually becoming more intrigued with her approach as they interact with students who have previously been in her classes. A few have been visiting her classroom. Mr. Apple is down the hall teaching his one semester of general biology together with a physical education unit that combined is called "Nutrition and Exercise." The students either jog or bicycle together, keep track of and modify their diets, monitor the nutritive elements and palatability of the school breakfast and lunch, modify their traditional family recipes, cook in class on a wok on a tripod stand over two Bunsen burners, but mostly carry out many inquiry biology investigations. He relates all concepts studied back to four big ideas in biology: homeostasis, growth and repair, ecosystems, and evolution/adaptation/reproduction. His students are learning to engage in respectful critical dialogue. He is not where Mrs. Thomas is in her understanding of how our brains learn and how to operationalize this in the classroom. However, he keeps visiting her "community of learners," and reading articles that she gives him as he engages in his own paradigm shift, his own cultural change, as his understanding of teaching and learning evolves. Likewise, second-grade teacher Ms. Egypt has been visiting Mrs. Thomas's classroom because she is using the same syringes with her FOSS *Air and Weather* kit. She realizes that her students cannot as yet identify and control variables and understand the complex properties of air in the way the ninth graders can, but much of the rest is directly applicable. She too has taken the plunge and is on her way to radically changing the culture of her classroom to align with what we know about how people learn.

Unfortunately, Marie's teacher and the other teachers in this school district did not have the opportunities afforded to Mrs. Thomas as she progressed through her university studies and into her initial teaching experiences. While an undergraduate, Mrs. Thomas experienced inquiry as a way of teaching and learning science, not only in her science methods classes, but also in two of her major's biology classes and in her student teaching. The professors who ran her preparation program were deeply familiar with current understandings about how students learn. Even more importantly, they had a commitment to overcome the pressures from local school districts to modify their "ivory tower" teachings and "unrealistic" expectations of preservice students and to convey the standard approaches used in schools. Instead, these professors worked long and hard in partnerships with school districts to create whole districts that were moving all their teachers toward practice similar to that used by Mrs. Thomas.

Mrs. Thomas did her student teaching in a real classroom where she could experience exemplary classroom interactions on a daily basis. She then began her teaching career working for two years in a district, before moving to her current teaching job, where the department chair had done a master's degree in science education—not just a master's degree in administration—that supported the same exemplary practices. This district had invested in nationally validated science curricula and kits, and most important, five years of sustained, effective staff development for all their science teachers. It was fertile ground for Mrs. Thomas to hone her craft.

It is twenty years into our latest round of science school reform, and most students are anxiously waiting for their Mrs. Thomas to emerge—for classroom instruction to align with our knowledge of how people learn.

References

Beaulieu, C., and Cynader, M. 1990. Effect of the richness of the environment on neurons in cat visual cortex. *Developmental Brain Research* 53: 71–78.

Bereiter, C., and Scardamalia, M. 1989. Intentional learning as a goal of instruction. In L. B. Resnick, ed., *Knowing, learning, and instruction*, 361–92. Hillsdale, NJ: Lawrence Erlbaum.

Bransford, J. D., Brown, A. L., and Cocking, R. R., eds. 1999. *How people learn: Brain, mind, experience, and school*. Washington, DC: National Academy Press.

Flick, L. B., Keys, C. W., Westbrook, S. L., Crawford, B. A., and Garnes, N. G. 1997. Perspectives on inquiry-oriented teaching practice: Conflict and clarification. Paper presented at the Annual Meeting of the National Association for Research in Science Teaching, March, Oakbrook, IL.

Lawson, A. E. 1995. *Science teaching and the development of thinking*. Belmont, CA: Wadsworth.

National Research Council (NRC). 1996. *National science education standards*. Washington, DC: National Academy Press.

Simon, H. A. 1980. Problem solving and education. In D. T. Tuma and R. Reif, eds., *Problem solving and education: Issues in teaching and research*, 81–96. Hillsdale, NJ: Lawrence Erlbaum.

Squire, L. R., and Kandel, E. R. 2000. *Memory from mind to molecules*. New York: Scientific American Library.

Tobin, K. 1990. Research on science laboratory activities: In pursuit of better questions and answers to improve learning. *School Science and Mathematics* 90(5): 403–18.

White, B.Y., and Frederickson, J. R. 1997. *The ThinkerTools Inquiry Project: Making scientific inquiry accessible to students*. Princeton, NJ: Center for Performance Assessment, Educational Testing Service.

———. 1998. Inquiry, modeling, and metacognition: Making science accessible to all students. *Cognition and Instruction* 16(1): 13–17.

Learner-Centered Teaching

Jeffrey Weld

Jeffrey Weld is an assistant professor of biology and science education at the University of Northern Iowa. A former high school biology teacher, he taught in the Rio Grande Valley of Texas, in suburban St. Louis, and in rural Iowa. Honors and awards as a high school teacher include the American Cyanamid Excellence in the Teaching of Science Award, an Access Excellence Fellowship of the Genentech Corporation, and the Focus on Excellence in Teaching Award of the Pella Corporation. He has written about science education innovation for *Phi Delta Kappan, Educational Leadership, The Science Teacher, The Journal of College Science Teaching, Educational Horizons, the Journal of Science Teacher Education,* and *Education Week.* He serves as a consultant for local, state, and national science education professional development initiatives.

There is a good deal of evidence that learning is enhanced when teachers pay attention to the knowledge and beliefs that learners bring to the learning task, use this knowledge as a starting point for new instruction, and monitor students' changing conceptions as instruction proceeds. (Bransford, Brown, and Cocking 2000, 11)

What on earth could science class possibly have to do with Ramiro Salinas? He lives for music—banging it out on a hand-me-down drum set or blasting his favorite CD, *Los Desperadoz*, out of his car window to an unappreciative neighborhood. Ramiro's parents operate a citrus grove where he earns enough money by picking and boxing grapefruit to replace a cymbal now and then. The grove will be his eventually. Ramiro doesn't see much point in nucleotide bases, vectors, balanced equations, lab reports, or science class.

Crystal Riggins sits next to Ramiro in science. This fortuitous arrangement allows them to chat discreetly or exchange notes about things that matter in their lives—weekend concerts, lunch options, the sunburn she incurred Saturday at Padre Island. Crystal's grandmother drives her to the island's wilderness preserve almost every weekend where they stroll in search of horseshoe crabs, abalone shells, and beached jellyfish. Crystal had considered becoming a marine biologist, but struggled to master dihybrid Punnett squares and cellular respiration last year in science. She's resolved that this would be the defining year, her last chance, to decide on scientific pursuits.

Jesse Garza sits two rows up and one over from Crystal and Ramiro. He's been anticipating this year for a long time, when he finally gets to go to Model Congress in Austin with the student government team. Jesse's family has never traveled beyond the Rio Grande Valley. They stay close to his father, a worker in a *maquiladora* factory across the river. Jesse is practically a father to his three younger siblings, and the experience steels his life goal of someday being a stay-at-home dad for his own children.

But in order to keep his options open, Jesse wants to keep his grades up by making sense of things like wave amplitude or directional selection or Bernoulli's Principle.

The Potency of Learning Theory

Learner-centered science teaching begins with the stories of learners. Who are they? What life experiences define them up to this point? What drives them? What are their hopes? What do they want to know? What do they need to know? Our recent wind-fall of knowledge about learning and teaching is a case of good news and bad news.

First, the good news: We know that answering those questions about our students can make science teaching vastly more effective. For it turns out that no one learns anything in a vacuum of mental engagement; there are no blank slates or empty vessels in our classrooms. Rather, each student has unique experience, beliefs, and conceptions (whether they be accurate or inaccurate) about the things we wish for them to learn. Or as Bransford, Brown, and Cocking (2000) phrase it in *How People Learn: Brain Mind, Experience, and School*, "All new learning involves transfer based on previous learning, and this fact has important implications for the design of instruction that helps students learn" (53). Recognizing and taking advantage of previous learning empowers teachers to do what has historically evaded us—reach all students.

Now the bad news: It takes considerable creative dedication for a teacher to break the mold in which science teaching has been cast since the dawn of formal schooling in America. The complex picture that has emerged from our present golden era of research on teaching and learning challenges all of us to re-examine our practices if not our goals, as well as our assumptions about students and science. It is a healthy process, this re-examination, which brings about an essential disequilibrium that Piaget considered a primary step in establishing new knowledge or beliefs. The advancement of teaching as a profession depends upon individual educators who frequently reflect on their own practices in light of accumulating knowledge about the nature of learning. Tough questions, some arising from within, others posed by the Teachers' Lounge Sage in every school, confront learner-centered educators:

◆ Does science class have to be fun to be meaningful?

◆ Like Ramiro, Crystal, and Jesse, every student is different—who has the time to get to know each student at a level that informs practice?

◆ How is one to ensure some standard of accountability in light of diverse talents and interests?

◆ Does this mean no more lectures?

◆ Does learner-centered teaching mean compromised content rigor for science class?

◆ Will any changes we make be superseded by the next curricular fad?

The answer to each question is… (drum roll, please, Ramiro), it depends on our goals for students. If we want authentic and meaningful learning—that is, usable knowledge rather than disconnected facts for each and every one of our students (Bransford, Brown, and Cocking 2000)—then modern learning theory needs to anchor our response to both practical and abstract questions about teaching. Again quoting Bransford, Brown, and Cocking (2000), "A benefit of focusing on how people learn is that it helps bring order to a seeming cacophony of choices" (21)—choices over both pedagogy and curriculum. Approaching our science classes from the vantage point of how it is that our students learn helps to make our teaching decisions clearer. Thus, when we are armed with knowledge as to how people learn and a commitment to being learner-center teachers, the answers to the above questions flow:

◆ Yes, it would help a great deal if our science classes were fun—interesting classes enhance motivation and motivation improves learning (Simpson, Koballa, and Oliver 1994).

◆ Since the experiences and attitudes of our students shape the way they craft usable knowledge in our science classes, and since there are a variety of attitudes and experiences among the students in our classes, we can't help but need to know these attitudes and experiences in order to be more effective teachers (Phillips 1994).

◆ A standard of accountability must be broadly defined as usable knowledge demonstrably evidenced on the part of individual students, who invoke unique talents and interests in using knowledge gained in their science classes (NRC 1996).

◆ Timely lectures are as effective for our students as they are for all of us—welcome at a point where we have a requisite competence to understand, and a curiosity that someone else can slake (Bransford, Brown, and Cocking 2000). The risk associated with lecture, however, is an assumption that Ramiro, Crystal, Jesse, and the rest of our students all arrive at an identical competence and curiosity at the time.

◆ Content rigor remains a vital force in the learner-centered science class, but must succeed rather than precede a foundation of critical thinking skill and interest among learners (Johnson and Lawson 1991). Facts then augment a scaffold upon which the process and new content of science can be assimilated (Bransford, Brown, and Cocking 2000). Learner-centered teaching recognizes that rigor is a relative notion dependent upon the interests and motivation of individuals, itself dependent on prior knowledge or experiences, and upon perceived relevance. Broadly imposed rigor for its own sake ignores the personal prescription each of our students deserves.

◆ The next curricular fad will be just as bound by learning theory as the last one. Examining educational innovations through a lens of how people learn breaks the fad cycle with which every thirty-year veteran of the classroom is all too familiar.

The potency of learning theory, like any theory borne of science, is that it not only explains so many observations of effective and ineffective learning, but that it also provides a framework for answering new questions. What can be expected of technology infusion in our science classrooms and laboratories? Of what value are expeditions and field trips for science students? What role should social issues play in a modern science class? How important is it that students connect what goes on in science class to what they learn in history, English, or physical education? A firm foundation in the central tenets of modern learning theory—cognitive development, account of prior experience, task meaningfulness, the value of social exchange, and on—enables science teachers to modulate the cacophony of curricular and peda-gogical choices. Now the question becomes "How?" How do informed teachers ac-count for learning theory in the daily classroom and laboratory milieu? Ramiro, Crys-tal, Jesse, and their classmates, just like students of science almost everywhere, endure a contrast in teacher styles that illustrates the as-yet incomplete metamorphosis of our profession.

The Science Tour

Mr. Diaz has planned for an upcoming unit on the subject of light. His goals for stu-dents—an awareness that light is a form of energy and has wave and particle proper-ties, an understanding of colors, reflection and refraction, and more—align with his district's curriculum guide as well as the content standards of the *National Science Education Standards* (NRC 1996). He sets about to sequence the events of a two-week unit. First, he schedules a retrospective lecture on the work of Thomas Young and Arthur Holly Compton that led to our current view that light can be particle-like or wavelike. Then, he will assign students to do a research paper on one of the contribu-tory historical figures on a list he has prepared. Meanwhile, in the laboratory, students will use mirrors to reflect a laser beam to pre-arranged targets. Toward week's end, Mr. Diaz will show what he considers an excellent video produced by the Electric Power Institute. On Friday, there'll be a quiz. The second week of the unit is to be launched with a Jeopardy-style questioning period on the category "light." Then he will lecture on the transmission and absorption of light, leading to the concept of color. A lab using prisms to measure index of refraction for various colors will ensue. Mr. Diaz has ar-ranged for a friend who works in the telecommunications industry to speak with his class about fiber optic voice and data transmission on Thursday, followed by the mul-tiple-choice unit test and research paper collection on Friday.

Mr. Diaz is hardly unique in his approach to science teaching. He operates his classroom like so many tour buses that depart the Rio Grande Valley for day trips through landmarks of northern Mexico and are back home in time for dinner. Tours typically begin promptly at dawn, ready or not. They wind through great northern cities like Monterrey and Saltillo, where the tourists are ushered off the bus to be hurried through the Tecaté brewery, or hustled up a Sierra Madre mountainside to view the Cola de Caballo (horsetail falls), then back to the bus for more sightseeing. The goal of the tour is coverage and efficiency.

Mr. Diaz's science tour follows a similarly frenetic pace in pursuit of coverage over substance. He makes an assumption that since his riders are present physically, no one missed the bus. But if they are with him at the start, students like Ramiro, Crystal, or Jesse might be looking to jump off before the tour's conclusion. Their interests, motivations, and capabilities are unaccounted for in Mr. Diaz's march through the subject of light. At three checkpoints Mr. Diaz assesses how much of what he's told them they can tell him back. If enough students recall enough of what he has covered, Mr. Diaz might consider the tour a success.

The Science Journey

Down the hall from Mr. Diaz, Mrs. Reyna also plans to launch a unit on light in her classroom. And like Mr. Diaz, her goals for students—an awareness that light is a form of energy and has wave and particle properties, an understanding of colors, reflection and refraction, and more—align with her district's curriculum guide as well as the Content Standards of the *National Science Education Standards (NSES)* (NRC 1996). Unlike Mr. Diaz, however, she also follows the recommendations of the Teaching Standards of the *NSES*, including planning "an inquiry-based science program for students" and "[managing] learning environments that provide students with the time, space, and resources needed for learning science" (NRC 1996, 20).

Mrs. Reyna budgets an entire month dedicated to the study of light. Though her vague and skeletal plans for the unit hardly fit the format of the school district's unit plan template, Mrs. Reyna is granted wide latitude by her administrators since educating them on the importance of flexibility for learner-centered teaching. She can only definitively say that Monday will be a brainstorming session spurred by some specific questions: How would your life be different without light? What sort of light is at work in your life? What do you know about light so far? What would you like to know? How could we find out? Mrs. Reyna has both a diagnosis and prescription from the class's first-day discussion. Jesse wants to know why newborn or premature infants are sometimes placed under ultraviolet lights. Ramiro is curious about a new kind of automobile headlight that gives off a blue rather than a yellow color. Crystal is curious about tanning-bed lights and their effect on our skin. Others express an interest in knowing more about human wake-sleep cycles and how light affects them, about solar power, how rainbows form, and whether someone could travel at the speed of light. Mrs. Reyna equips a corner of the laboratory with Web-accessible computers and a collection of relevant books, articles, and leaflets. She and the students gather equipment and material for conducting a broad variety of investigations.

The remaining days and weeks of the unit unfold in a flurry of activity: student groups arrange for electronic or personal interviews with physicians, mechanics, and college professors. They conduct experiments on the effect of tanning-bed light on the growth of simple organisms, on the growth of plants subjected to different light sources, and on themselves trying to sleep with the lights on. They build models, conduct library and Internet research, hold class debates, invite community experts to visit their class. Finally they share all that they've found in the form of reports, multimedia displays, role plays, or action plans.

If Mrs. Reyna were running the tour bus, no one would be hurried through Monterrey's Tecaté brewery or the Cola de Caballo. The tour would be more like a journey, commencing from whatever starting point the students find themselves. Then their journey builds, detours, revisits, and explores according to the tastes and abilities of the riders. But by the time this tour group winds its way through northern Mexico, their knowledge of the place, and their interest in its culture and content, is far deeper than that of their whirlwind counterparts.

And the same is true for science. Students who enjoy a personalized, deeper, more open exploratory tour of science consistently outperform their traditionally taught peers on even traditionally designed standardized content assessments (Myers 1996). In addition, they make gains in areas such as science process skills, creativity, confidence, and attitudes about science (Weld 1999).

The Learner-Centered Teacher: A Map and a Mirror

Learner-centered teachers are in the driver's seat of their science classrooms, calling upon a professional knowledge base of subject matter content, learner characteristics, and pedagogical skills to facilitate student learning. But steering a learner-centered science class requires close monitoring of the map and the mirror.

The map that guides a learner-centered environment details science landmarks—essential knowledge and skills as described in the *National Science Education Standards* (NRC 1996) and in Project 2061's *Benchmarks for Science Literacy* (AAAS 1993). But it also includes the various routes one might take toward those destinations according to the strengths and interests of learners. And it is the interest and background of each individual learner that helps make decisions about effective routes toward goals. It takes a genuine pro to effectively navigate by a learner-centered map.

The mirror used by learner-centered teachers accommodates constant reflection on student learning, and on teacher teaching. By using their mirror to look back on what they teach, how they teach it, and to whom they teach, reflective science teachers re-evaluate and reform their existing theories about teaching and about learners in light of what Abell and Bryan (1997) call "perturbing evidence." The mirror reveals perturbing evidence in the form of new research findings, novel educational methods, student dynamics, school political changes, and so on, to which teachers need to adjust.

Learner-centered science class environments must, by virtue of the nature of learning, take circuitous routes. But they are carefully monitored by a professional educator armed with a map and a mirror.

Destinations

Students like Ramiro, Crystal, and Jesse populate each of our classes. Like all humans, they are naturally curious and biologically endowed with sense-making capabilities. We know vastly more about how they learn—tapping their curiosity, working within their sense-making schemes—than did our own school teachers just a decade or two ago. This new knowledge has both complicated and clarified the art and craft of science teaching. Perhaps most notably, it has brought to the fore the importance of getting to know our students: How do they think? What do they know? Why should they care? The Ramiro Salinas in each of our classrooms can and should learn our science, but it will most surely be on his terms. The Jesse Garza we all know has the motivation and inclination, but awaits inspiration. And the Crystal Riggins in every science class deserves to know science as relevant to her life and career ambitions. This year perhaps they will all have learner-centered science teachers.

References

Abell, S. K., and Bryan, L. A. 1997. Reconceptualizing the elementary science methods course using a reflection orientation. *Journal of Science Teacher Education* 8 (3): 153–66.

American Association for the Advancement of Science (AAAS). 1993. *Benchmarks for science literacy.* Washington, DC: AAAS.

Bransford, J. D., Brown, A. L., and Cocking, R. R., eds. 2000. *How people learn: Brain, mind, experience, and school.* Washington, DC: National Academy Press.

Johnson, M. A., and Lawson, A. E. 1991. What are the relative effects of reasoning ability and prior knowledge on biology achievement in expository and inquiry classes? *Journal of Research in Science Teaching* 35 (1): 89–103.

Myers, L. 1996. Mastery of basic concepts. In Yager, R. E., ed., *Science/technology/society as reform in science education*, 53–58. Albany, NY: SUNY Press.

National Research Council (NRC). 1996. *National science education standards.* Washington, DC: National Academy Press.

Phillips, D. 1994. *Sciencing toward logical thinking.* Dubuque, IA: Kendall/Hunt.

Simpson, R. D., Koballa, T. R., Jr., and Oliver, J. S. 1994. Research on the affective dimension of science learning. In Gabel, D. L., ed., *Handbook of research in science teaching and learning*, 211–34. New York: Macmillan.

Weld, J. 1999. Achieving equitable science education: It isn't rocket science. *Phi Delta Kappan* 80 (10): 756–58.

Using the Laboratory to Enhance Student Learning

Michael P. Clough

Michael P. Clough is an assistant professor in the Center for Excellence in Science and Mathematics Education at Iowa State University. Before coming to Iowa State, he was an assistant professor at the University of Iowa, where he directed a nationally recognized model preservice science teacher education program. He taught high school biology and chemistry for seven years in Illinois and Wisconsin and was recognized for effective science teaching with a National Tandy Scholar Outstanding Science Teacher Award and Wisconsin Society of Science Teachers Regional Award for Excellence in Science Education. He has published widely and given numerous presentations concerning effective teaching; many of his publications and presentations address the modification of science activities so they are more consistent with the *National Science Education Standards*, how students learn, and the nature of science.

There are important differences between tasks and projects that encourage hands-on doing and those that encourage doing with understanding….
(Bransford, Brown, and Cocking 2000, 24).

In *Alice in Wonderland*, Alice asks which way she should go, and is told, "That depends a good deal on where you want to get to." Similarly, before addressing the role of laboratory experiences, where we wish to take students must first be articulated. For instance, developing deep, robust, and long-term understanding of science concepts is one aim of the *National Science Education Standards* (NRC 1996), but the vision also includes an understanding of the nature of science and the attributes and skills that make for effective science inquiry. NSTA's popular *Focus on Excellence* monograph series (Bonnstetter, Penick, and Yager 1983; Penick 1983a, 1983b; Penick and Bonnstetter 1983; Penick and Lunetta 1984; Penick and Meinhard-Pellens 1984) suggested that the goals listed below were commonly associated with exemplary science teaching:

◆ Convey self-confidence and a positive self-image.

◆ Use critical thinking skills.

◆ Convey an understanding of the nature(s) of science.

◆ Identify and solve problems effectively.

◆ Use communication and cooperative skills effectively.

◆ Actively participate in working toward solutions to local, national, and global problems.

◆ Be creative and curious.

◆ Set goals, make decisions, and self-evaluate.

◆ Convey a positive attitude about science.

◆ Access, retrieve, and use the existing body of scientific knowledge in the process of investigating phenomena.

◆ Demonstrate deep understanding of science concepts.

◆ Demonstrate an awareness of the importance of science in many careers.

The task is formidable and reaching these lofty goals will not occur without rethinking laboratory activities and the role of the teacher so they reflect how people learn and promote student actions consistent with the desired state set forth in the *National Science Education Standards* (NRC 1996) and *NSTA Pathways to the Science Standards, High School Edition* (Texley and Wild 1996).

How People Learn

Science teachers are well aware that even when they explain ideas slowly, carefully, and clearly, students often fail to grasp the intended meaning. Understanding how students learn—and why they often struggle to grasp our intended meaning—is the foundation of informed teaching. To achieve robust long-term understanding, multiple connections must be erected and grounded in experience, but unfortunately these links cannot simply be given to students. Fundamental to our understanding of learning is that students must be mentally active—selectively taking in and attending to information, and connecting and comparing it to prior knowledge in an attempt to make sense of what is being received. However, in attempting to make sense of instruction, students often interpret and sometimes modify incoming stimuli so that it fits (i.e., connects) to what they already believe. Consequently, students' prior knowledge that is at odds with intended learning can be incredibly resistant to change. Driver (1997) argued that

> *some of the more complicated learning we have to do in life, and a lot of science is like this, involves not adding new information to what we already know, but changing the way we think about the information we already have. It means developing new ways of seeing things.*

Toward this end, effective laboratory experiences are highly interactive and make explicit students' relevant prior knowledge, engender active mental struggling with that prior knowledge and new experiences, and encourage metacognition. Without this, students will rarely create meaning similar to that of the scientific community. That is why typical cookbook laboratory activities do not promote, and often hinder, deep conceptual understanding; they do an extremely poor job of making apparent and playing off students' prior ideas, engendering deep reflection, and promoting understanding of complex content. Such activities mask students' underlying beliefs and make desired learning outcomes difficult to achieve.

Hands-On Is Not Enough

For decades, hands-on experiences have been promoted as the solution to helping students learn science. That direct experience will improve students' understanding seems intuitively obvious, but evidence indicates that such experiences, by themselves, do not lead to a scientific understanding of the natural world. In *Minds of Our Own* (1997) college graduates, despite their everyday hands-on experience with mirrors, incorrectly state that if they move closer to or further away from a mirror in which they can see only half their body, then they will be able to see their entire reflection. A barber who spends his days in front of a mirror conveys the same misconception, illustrating that experience alone is insufficient for developing a scientific point of view. Such experiences, like cookbook laboratory activities, do not force us to confront a different way of looking at the mirror. Hands-on experiences, by themselves, are insufficient for coming to an understanding of the scientific community's explanation for natural phenomena—students must also be mentally engaged. Pre-fabricated cookbook activities, so ubiquitous in science teaching, rarely engage students in ways necessary to facilitate such an understanding. As Bransford, Brown, and Cocking (2000) write, "Hands-on experiments *can* be a powerful way to ground emergent knowledge, but they do not alone evoke the underlying conceptual understandings that aid generalization" (22).

To understand why traditional hands-on experiences fail to meaningfully engage students, consider the following questions that must be asked in authentic scientific inquiry:

◆ What is known and what questions are raised by this knowledge?

◆ What investigative procedure will address particular questions?

◆ What equipment is necessary to carry out this procedure?

◆ What data is relevant and should be collected?

◆ How will the data be analyzed?

◆ What does the data mean?

◆ What mathematical calculations, if any, are required and in which order should they occur?

◆ How is the work to be communicated to readers?

In typical cookbook laboratory experiences, most all these decisions are made *for* students. Not only does this misportray the nature of scientific inquiry, but because most all the thinking is done for students they have little reason to engage in the cognitive activities known to be essential for robust learning (e.g. selectively considering and attending to information and comparing it to prior knowledge). Moreover, teachers get a poor picture of what students know and can do, which hinders dialogue and lesson planning that would deliberately move students to that desired learning. Using the laboratory to enhance student learning requires a reconceptualization of science activities.

Restructuring Science Activities

Saunders (1992) noted that

> *[c]ognitive activities such as thinking out loud, developing alternative explanations, interpreting data, participating in cognitive conflict (constructive argumentation about phenomena under study), development of alternative hypotheses, the design of further experiments to test alternative hypotheses, and the selection of plausible hypotheses from among competing explanations are all examples of learner activities which [mentally engage students].* (140)

However, science teachers are far too busy to invent every laboratory experience from scratch so that they are more consistent with how students learn and so that they reflect desired goals for students, the *National Science Education Standards*, and the nature of science. As Clark, Clough, and Berg (2000) state,

> *In rethinking laboratory activities, too often a false dichotomy is presented to teachers that students must either passively follow a cookbook laboratory procedure or, at the other extreme, investigate a question of their own choosing. These extremes miss the large and fertile middle ground that is typically more pedagogically sound than either end of the continuum.* (40)

They suggested that effective laboratory experiences can be created by modifying existing activities so they make explicit students' relevant prior knowledge, engender active mental struggling with that prior knowledge and new experiences, and encourage metacognition. To illustrate this, they presented in some detail how the common cookbook laboratory activity addressing the mass percent of water in a hydrate was altered so that students engaged in the cognitive activities essential for active learning. In an earlier article, Clough and Clark (1994a) presented a cookbook laboratory activity they had picked up at an NSTA national convention and showed how they modified it to ascertain their students' prior knowledge, require metacognition, and confront a common chemistry misconception.

When modifying traditional laboratory activities into experiences that are far more likely to promote learning and other important goals we have for students, teachers should:

1. Require students to make explicit their prior knowledge.

2. Structure and scaffold activities so that students must access and employ previously studied science ideas——that is, ensure that activities reflect a spiraling curriculum.

3. Determine whether the experience is to be primarily an exploratory or application activity.

4. Where appropriate, include students in setting the lab question to be investigated.

5. Where appropriate, have students invent laboratory procedures (consider safety, equipment, and cognitive issues).

6. When students cannot invent laboratory procedures, structure the experience so students *must* be mentally engaged in the lab.

7. Use materials and equipment that are no more complex than necessary.

8. Force students to consider and defend what data are relevant and irrelevant.

9. Have students decide what their data means.

10. Require students to apply mathematical reasoning to problems.

11. Make students responsible for communicating their lab work in a clear manner.

12. Have students set goals, make decisions, and assess progress.

13. Ask questions that spark ideas and reduce student frustration.

14. Refrain from summative evaluations of students' ideas and interpretations.

Most of these suggestions are illustrated in articles appearing in *The Science Teacher* (Clough and Clark 1994a, 1994b; Colburn and Clough 1997; Clark, Clough, and Berg 2000), but three require further discussion here. For instance, how does exchanging complex laboratory equipment with more simple everyday materials promote learning? When equipment (even when it is not particularly complex) is used before students have seriously grappled with the concepts under study, they often incorrectly assume that the equipment is an essential part of the concept. For instance, after students used a bulb holder in a batteries and bulb activity to illustrate circuits, interviewers (*Minds of Our Own* 1997) found that one of the brightest students in the honors physics class thought the bulb holder was a necessary part of a circuit. The presence of this rudimentary piece of equipment and its "black box" nature not only clouded the purpose of the bulb holder but also created a misconception regarding the basic concept of a circuit, upon which many other science concepts are built. In redesigning laboratory experiences, care must be taken to avoid using equipment too far removed from students' conceptual understanding. As with science concepts, teachers need to scaffold the use of science equipment so that students grasp what the equipment is doing for them and do not mistakenly couple the equipment to the concept.

Another consideration in modifying activities is deciding whether the redesigned experience is to serve primarily as an exploratory or application activity. If activities are appropriately scaffolded, then explorations will require students to apply previously addressed concepts even though the chief purpose of the modified activity is to ensure that students have relevant and concrete experiences prior to discussing science concepts illustrated in the activity. In these cases, laboratory modifications emphasize having direct experience precede verbal instruction so that students will bring to the surface their prior knowledge, raise questions, and connect future verbal abstractions to the concrete experiences. When modifying laboratory activities to serve as applications, changes should be made with the primary purpose of having students use what they have learned in unique situations.

What to do when students, for either safety or cognitive reasons, must follow a step-by-step procedure appears to be a vexing problem in promoting more effective laboratory experiences. The solution is to structure these experiences so students *must* be mentally engaged while following the given procedure. A number of ways exist to do this, but an easy change is simply to pose questions at each step of a procedure that forces students to consider the rationale for the step. Below are just a few examples of questions I inserted (italicized) in a traditional step-by-step procedure my students followed to determine the heat of combustion of a candle.

1. Determine and record the mass of an empty 12 oz soda can. *What is the importance of determining the mass of the can? What about a 12 oz soda can makes it particularly suited for this experiment?*

2. Add 90–100 mL of water to the soda can. Drop small pieces of ice into the soda can a few at a time until the temperature of the water is lowered to 9º to 10ºC below room temperature. Be very careful not to allow the temperature to fall any lower than this. Remove any unmelted ice. *What is the significance of 90–100 mL? What is the rationale for lowering the water temperature 9º to 10ºC below room temperature? How would the results be different if you lowered the temperature a different amount?*

3. Weigh the can plus the water. Record this mass. *What is the importance of weighing the can again?*

4. Place the candle under the can of water and light the candle. Stir the water gently with a stirring rod as it heats. *How would not stirring the water affect your results? What error is being introduced by stirring the water with a stirring rod? Why stir the water gently rather than briskly?*

5. Continue heating until the temperature rises as far above room temperature as it was below room temperature at the start of the experiment. *What is the rationale for heating the water as far above room temperature as it was below room temperature at the start of the experiment? What would happen if you didn't?*

Such questions are not trivial because they force students to engage mentally in understanding the laboratory design and science concept being investigated. For instance, my students were bewildered at my question regarding the 12 oz soda can, seeing it as simply a container for water. After I asked additional questions, they made the connection that the thin aluminum wall of the can was important in maintaining, within reason, that heat lost by the candle is gained by the water—a critical conceptual claim in the experiment. Understandably, the approaches suggested above are initially frustrating to students accustomed to thoughtlessly following directions, and consequently, the role of the teacher is pivotal for engaging students in a manner reflecting how we know people learn.

The Critical Role of the Teacher

Such modifications make the teacher's role in student learning far more critical, for without well-reasoned teacher intervention in both the designed lab structure and its implementation, students will become frustrated because alone, they will rarely create meaning similar to that of the scientific community. Science ideas appear obvious once a deep and accurate understanding exists, but for students in the midst of piecing together such understanding, it is not at all obvious! Without a teacher's perceptive questioning and responding that plays off students' observations, actions, and thinking, they would rarely put together intended ideas in an accurate fashion. This intervention is considerably different than that occurring in most science classrooms today (Penick 1991) and reflects a different perspective on how people learn. Sympathizing with the difficult task of understanding how people learn and the need to change the teacher's role, Driver (1997) stated that

> our optimism about what children ought to be able to do stems perhaps from rather deep-seated views about learning. And that as long as the expert tells the story clearly and that the person who is learning is listening and paying attention then they will automatically build up the understanding that the expert has. Now all our current knowledge in cognitive science, and in cognitive psychology, and in science education is telling us that simply does not happen. Children may well be listening, paying attention to what is being said or what they are reading in a book, but they are construing it in different ways to the ways that the teacher intended. And that is the issue we have to deal with.

However, the already overwhelming demands placed on teachers make difficult the learning and introduction of new teaching strategies. Fortunately, the gentle approach to changing laboratory activities also applies to changing the teacher's role in those activities. By gradually shifting to the new strategies and teaching behaviors listed below, as advocated by Colburn and Clough (1997), teachers and students can become accustomed to new roles with less stress.

1. Conduct an exploratory lab experience prior to verbally introducing content.

   ◆ Increases interest

   ◆ Reflects how we tend to learn

2. Discuss the lab before verbally introducing content.

   ◆ Increases interest in the interactive information presentation that follows

   ◆ Reflects how we tend to learn

3. Require students to decide how lab findings will be communicated.

   ◆ Requires students to think and be creative

   ◆ Reduces boredom of reviewing students' lab reports

4. Change the test.

   ◆ Assessment should reflect the course goals

   ◆ Students place importance on what is being assessed

5. Begin changing your role during the activity.

   ◆ Essential core of effective teaching (Effective questioning, wait-time, encouraging nonverbal behaviors, listening, and nonevaluative responding)

   ◆ This is the most difficult step as patterns are difficult to change

6. Have students invent the procedures to answer a lab question.

   ◆ The teacher's role is critical (high expectations require high support)

   ◆ Most of the decisions about how to answer a question must be on the students' shoulders, but the teacher's role is critical in supporting students

7. Continue changing your role during the lab activity.

   ◆ Keep working to implement the essential core

   ◆ Audiotaping and videotaping are crucial for advancing practice

8. Employ application lab experiences so students must use what they learn in new contexts.

   ◆ Inquiry now reflects what students have learned

   ◆ Inability to apply often indicates lack of understanding

   ◆ Some application activities also serve as exploratory activities for further learning

9. Have students invent lab questions and procedures.

  ◆ May only occur once or twice in a school year and makes for an excellent year-end final exam

  ◆ May simply be hypothetical

Modifying the structure of preexisting cookbook labs, asking effective questions, incorporating appropriate wait-time, carefully listening, acknowledging and playing off student ideas, and exhibiting positive nonverbal behavior (e.g., smiling, maintaining eye contact, leaning forward when students are speaking, raising eyebrows to show interest) are all key for creating the mentally engaging and productive environment conducive to learning.

The end result appears to a layperson as simply hands-on learning, but to the expert teacher who is sensitive to the intricacies of learning, it is far more complex than that. Both the student and teacher are thinking, but on different planes. The most significant difference is that while *students* are connecting these hands-on experiences to their current and emerging conceptual framework, the *teacher* is desperately trying to understand students' thinking to further engage them in that construction of knowledge. Hence, placing greater responsibility on students does not mean simply having them figure things out on their own. Rather than abdicating responsibility for teaching, an understanding of how people learn demands from teachers a far more complex and demanding role in promoting students' understanding of science.

References

Bonnstetter, R. J., Penick, J. E., and Yager, R. E. 1983. *Teachers in exemplary programs: How do they compare?* Washington, DC: National Science Teachers Association.

Bransford, J. D., Brown, A. L., and Cocking, R. R., eds. 2000. *How people learn: Brain, mind, experience, and school.* Washington, DC: National Academy Press.

Clark, R. L., Clough, M. P., and Berg, C. A. 2000. Modifying cookbook labs: A different way of teaching a standard laboratory engages students and promotes understanding. *The Science Teacher* 67 (7): 40–43.

Clough, M. P., and Clark, R. L. 1994a. Cookbooks and constructivism: A better approach to laboratory activities. *The Science Teacher* 61 (2): 34–37.

———. 1994b. Creative constructivism: Challenge your students with an authentic science experience. *The Science Teacher* 61(7): 46–49.

Colburn, A., and Clough, M. P. 1997. Implementing the learning cycle. *The Science Teacher* 64 (5): 30–33.

Driver, R. 1997. In Annenberg/CPB *Minds of Our Own VideotapeProgram One: Can We Believe Our Eyes*, Math and Science Collection, P.O. Box 2345, South Burlington, VT 05407-2345.

Minds of Our Own. 1997. *VideotapeProgram One: Can We Believe Our Eyes*, Annenberg/CPB Math and Science Collection, P.O. Box 2345, South Burlington, VT 05407-2345.

National Research Council (NRC). 1996. *National science education standards.* Washington, DC: National Academy Press.

Penick, J. E. 1983a. *Focus on excellence: Science as inquiry.* Washington, DC: National Science

Teachers Association.

———. 1983b. *Focus on excellence: Elementary science*. Washington, DC: National Science Teachers Association.

———. 1991. Where's the science? *The Science Teacher* 58 (5): 26–29.

Penick, J. E., and Bonnstetter, eds. 1983. *Focus on excellence: Biology*. Washington, DC: National Science Teachers Association.

Penick, J. E., and Lunetta, V. N. 1984. *Focus on excellence: Physical science*. Washington, DC: National Science Teachers Association.

Penick, J. E., and Meinhard-Pellens, R., eds. 1984. *Focus on excellence: Science/technology/society*. Washington, DC: National Science Teachers Association.

Saunders, W. L. 1992. The constructivist perspective: Implications and teaching strategies for science. *School Science and Mathematics* 92 (3): 136–41.

Texley, J., and Wild, A. 1996. *NSTA pathways to the science standards: Guidelines for moving the vision into practice* (high school edition). Arlington, VA: National Science Teachers Association.

PART 4

Assessing Student Learning

Using Assessment to Help Students Learn

J. Myron Atkin

J. Myron (Mike) Atkin is a professor of education and human biology at Stanford University. He is principal investigator for an National Science Foundation (NSF)–supported research project on how middle school science teachers improve their assessment practices to help students learn. He currently chairs the Committee on Science Education K–12 at the National Research Council (NRC) and formerly chaired the NRC committee that prepared an addendum to the *National Science Education Standards* on assessment in the science classroom. He taught science for seven years in New York elementary and secondary schools, co-directed a curriculum development project on astronomy, and has been dean of education at the University of Illinois at Urbana-Champaign and at Stanford.

In addition to being learner centered and knowledge centered, effectively designed learning environments must also be assessment centered.
(Bransford, Brown, and Cocking 1999, 128)

Scores of assessments happen every day in every classroom. Usually there are dozens every hour. The teacher asks a question. A student interprets the question, and responds. The teacher makes a judgment about how well the student understands. All the other students listening to the exchange also interpret what the teacher was asking, and they also evaluate the quality of the response. Frequently they make a comparison with how they might have answered the same question.

Consider this example: Two third-graders explain their experiments with snails to the other students in the class. They had investigated certain aspects of snail behavior by trying to find out how snails react to light and dark. Do the snails move toward light or away from it? The two students also had become interested in how snails navigate obstacles, like rocks, and so tried some experiments. Several students and the teacher question the two presenters closely about the report of their experiments. Does the brightness of the light make a difference? What about the size and shape of the rock? Everyone in the room is hard at work trying to figure out just how the experiments demonstrate something important about the behavior of snails.

The responses to most of their classmates' questions indicate how well the two presenters understand the concepts they are trying to demonstrate. But by their questions, those who ask them are also revealing their levels of understanding about the effect of light and dark on how snails move to. The questions, answers, and discussion, in fact, lead to further questions not only about the direction of snail movement but its speed—including discussion of how fast snails move on different surfaces.

The author is grateful to Janet Coffey for her suggestions about a draft of this chapter.

New experiments were designed by the entire class to investigate snail behavior further.

Previously the teacher had worked with the third-graders to develop guidelines for making presentations. They had been summarized on a chart:

◆ What did you do?

◆ What did you find?

◆ How might you have done it differently?

◆ What questions do you now have?

The teacher and students had also talked about evaluating oral presentations: Are the main ideas clear? (And what does it mean to be clear?) Is the presentation interesting? (And why is being "interesting" important?) Do the presenters know their subject? (For example, what can they say about how snails propel themselves?) Do the presenters respond directly to the questions? Do they provide evidence for their conclusions? Do they tell the class when they don't know an answer—or when they aren't sure? For about twenty minutes after the presentation, there is an assessment-rich discussion in the class about snail behavior under different conditions, about the originality and adequacy of the experiments, and about the quality of the presentation. These kinds of appraisals are part of almost every teaching situation.

Teachers also use more formal assessments—for example, written or oral weekly quizzes, end-of-semester examinations, and comments and/or grades on homework assignments. In fact, these are the formats that usually come to mind when thinking about assessment in the classroom. However, both informal and formal classroom-assessment procedures are seen everywhere as teachers work with students, and as students work with each other. Together, they serve several purposes: to help students learn, to illustrate and articulate the standards for quality work, to inform teaching, and to provide a basis for reporting concrete accomplishments to parents.

Of course these aren't the only kinds of assessment in school. For many people, in fact, they pale in importance to the many standardized examinations that are administered in the course of a student's life. These include periodic tests required by the state department of education throughout the elementary and secondary school years, Advanced Placement examinations, and college-entrance exams. Such tests are designed not primarily to improve learning or teaching, but to certify that students have attained certain levels of proficiency or to serve as a measure of school or teacher accountability. Each of these assessments—in-class procedures and tests administered by external agencies—serves a specific purpose. But none of them, alone, can fulfill all the possible or desired aims of gauging students' knowledge and abilities. Few of the commonly used and widely known assessment instruments that are developed outside the classroom help students get better at their work in school. Most of them don't even help students understand the ways in which they were judged to fall short because the standardized tests devised by people outside the school usually are given at the end of a year or course, with no feedback provided to teacher or student about the nature of their errors or what they can do about them. For the students as well as the adults, in fact, the score serves mainly as a means of judging and sorting. This student is college "material." That one is not. This one is an "A." This one is a "C."

Formative Assessment

Assessments in the classroom that usually take place in the course of the *ongoing, daily lives of teachers and their students*, like the ones in the third-grade class studying snails, are often called "formative" because they can be used directly to improve learning. Such assessment is the focus of this chapter.

Consider an example with older students: Three high-school juniors are working on an environmental-analysis project and are trying to determine the range of plant species living in a nearby, overgrown three-acre lot. How should they go about it? What fraction of the lot should they sample if they want to say something about the entire lot? How should they select the sample(s)? Should they go beneath the surface, and if so how deeply? Does the season matter? What methods should they use?

This investigation by the three students is part of a project in which the entire class is conducting a survey of living organisms in the lot. The project was selected because the city council is debating whether to authorize construction of a parking lot on that piece of land. Environmental impact is important not only to the students but also to the entire community. Some of their classmates are working on other aspects of the investigation: a census of animals, the amount and consequences of water run-off, and possible pollution from grease and oil from the automobiles that will be parked there. The teacher comes to the group working on the variety of plant species. The students tell her what they are doing. She asks what they know about the lot already. Do there seem to be different conditions in different parts of the lot? The group isn't sure what she means. "Do some parts get more sunlight?" she asks. "Would that make a difference in deciding about samples? Are there other factors?" The students begin talking among themselves about the questions she raised.

Such assessments are ubiquitous in classrooms, and frequent. And they serve many purposes. In the above exchange between teacher and students, the teacher's first question is designed to find out what the students already know. But her follow-up questions gradually shift to several that are designed as much to teach as to assess their knowledge. In the case of the third-grade students' presentation on snail behavior, the comments of those in the audience serve to indicate how well the presenters conveyed their main ideas and how well they are understood by the class. Yet the ensuing discussion, focused on assessment, also teaches the students in a concrete fashion about the quality of work that is expected in the class.

Almost every exchange among students about their work, and between teacher and students, is an occasion for an assessment. In fact assessment is such a natural feature of teaching and learning that it blends in with all other aspects of classroom life. Everyone involved in education, of themselves or of others, does it again and again. Although few students or teachers when asked to describe their assessment activities would include such exchanges, the examples make evident the intimate connection between teaching and assessment. It is difficult, in fact, to separate the two. The third-graders who designed experiments on snail behavior are generally pleased with the originality of their ideas. They seem especially proud of having thought of the plan to use rocks of different shapes, with sides of different slopes, to study snail navigation. They also are pleased about the way in which they designed a long box that was lighted at one end and dark at the other. But as the class discusses their experiments, some students ask about the effect of the heat from the light bulb on the snails' movements. Is it light or heat—or a combination—that caused the snails to move as they did?

This question highlights the fact that assessment is embedded in science itself. Those engaged in scientific inquiry continually make judgments about how well their conclusions follow from the evidence they have collected. The comment about the effects of heat leads to a discussion about how a device might be designed in which the effects of heat and light could be studied independently. Thus the students are doing science as they are assessing the quality of their classmates' report. They are identifying new questions as they gain greater understanding of the old ones. There is a trajectory to their inquiries about animal behavior that has the potential for further study and deeper understanding.

There are several key features of formative assessment, which can be summarized as follows:

◆ The goal or goals of the lesson or project must be clear to the student. (What learning is expected?)

◆ The student must begin to understand his or her current levels of understanding with respect to the goals. (What is the gap between current understanding and the concept to be learned?)

◆ As the student tries to close the gap between the goal and current understanding, feedback is necessary to help the student understand the reasons for his or her progress, or lack of it. (Where did the student make an error or where might another approach have been taken to the task?)

◆ It is the quality of the feedback, rather than its absence or presence, that is central. Does the feedback help the student understand what must be done to improve? (Urging the student to "try harder" is much less helpful than leading the student to an understanding of the source of confusion.)

◆ The student must be able to use the feedback and take action on the basis of the new information.

◆ Student participation in classroom assessment is a key component at every step of the process.

As noted in Bransford, Brown, and Cocking (1999), "The key principles of assessment are that they should provide opportunities for feedback and revision and that what is assessed must be congruent with one's learning goals" (128).

Peer- and Self-Assessment by Students

New developments in the science of learning also emphasize the importance of helping people to take control of their own learning. Since understanding is viewed as important, people must learn to recognize when they understand and when they need more information. (Bransford, Brown, and Cocking 1999, 10)

The vignettes about studies of snail behavior and biological diversity illustrate practices that many teachers use regularly: listening carefully to students' comments and questions, asking follow-up questions, helping students understand the characteristics of quality work, and engaging students in evaluation of the work being examined. In many ways, this last point—student self-assessment—is the heart of the matter. To make continual progress as a learner, one must gradually wean oneself from dependency on the comments of others. However useful and necessary teachers and coaches are, they are not usually available on a continuing basis to guide and direct. Successful self-monitoring is the most prevalent form of learning.

One way that some teachers promote self-assessment skills is to develop assessment guidelines, often in the form of "rubrics," with their students. For the snail-behavior presentation, the teacher had worked with the entire class developing a general framework by which presentations could be assessed. (Are the procedures used in the investigation described adequately? What did you find out? Are the main ideas clear? Do the presenters seem to know their subject? Do the presenters tell the class when they don't know the answer to a question?) Afterward, the entire class participated in the assessment. As the teacher revised this type of rubric construction over a period of several years, she developed a pattern of first asking the students who made the presentation to comment on the quality of the work. Thus assessment by peers was integrated gradually with student self-assessment.

Some teachers use work completed by students in past years to provide a basis for discussions of standards and quality in the current class. A teacher introduces lab reports as a new assignment in her sixth-grade class, for example. She has saved examples of student work from past years. She selects several (minus student identification) to show to the new group, and the class is asked to evaluate them. Is Report A an example of good work? Why? What might have been done to Report B to improve it? Would this have been a reasonable request to make of the student? What information might have helped the student who prepared Report B do a better job?

Conversations of this kind hone perceptions of quality. They help the students just starting with a new task develop a sense of what is expected, what constitutes work that is of higher and lesser quality, and why. The use of prior work by other students also avoids putting pressure on any student in the current class. Teachers attracted to this aspect of assessment want each student to be able eventually to accept and use criticism, however; doing so is part of science, just as it is a part of formative assessment. But analysis of anonymous work makes the conversation less personal and more candid.

After this kind of activity, students can begin to examine each other's work in progress. In one eighth-grade class, students operate in pairs, critiquing each other's work. First, Student A comments on Student B's diagram, written observations, or lab write-up. Student B has an opportunity to make changes, but she also has an occasion, later, to comment on how useful the feedback was. For another assignment, the two students reverse roles. This sort of peer assessment, again, is part of science as well as a way to improve self-assessment skills.

In classrooms such as those discussed here, learning is not viewed as solely an individual activity. Teachers and students develop shared understandings of standards for quality work. The assessment conversations come to be seen as embedded in the fabric of classroom life, not like a quiz at the end of the week or a special examination. This approach is consistent with the emphasis some researchers place on metacognition (thinking about thinking) and the related idea that a role of the teacher is to provide "scaffolding" for learning (an intellectual framework to which new ideas might be related). It isn't always necessary to follow a particular series of assessment steps in a formal or sequential way when actually teaching. In the ordinary give-and-take of classroom life, opportunities arise unexpectedly to reexamine the goal of learning or to revisit a student's current understanding of a concept.

Formative assessment cannot be implemented well without serious attention to the nature and level of the subject matter to be taught. It is not disembodied from the curriculum itself. Which concepts are most important, and for what reasons? Are some ideas particularly fruitful for laying the foundations for further learning? Are some of them more closely related than others to what the students already know and thus can be presumed to be more accessible? To assess well for purposes of helping students to learn, it is necessary to identify priorities for the science class. As has been noted, carefully identified goals are essential, even if pedagogical circumstances necessitate modification. Recall the teacher talking with the three students investigating biological diversity in the vacant lot. On the basis of the information she gleans in the brief conversation, she raises some questions she believes will help the group think more productively about what they might do next. She may not have identified all the specific content areas in advance, but she wants the students to think about how they might take constructive action to increase their own knowledge of the particular scientific concepts that have arisen.

The science teacher, in choosing a main content goal and the associated intermediate goals that may be steppingstones toward understanding that goal, will be exercising subject expertise—by commitment to certain aims for learning science, by knowing the science concepts that best relate to that goal, and by professional understanding of the ways by which students progress in understanding the concepts and skills that lead to those goals. To do this well, the teacher needs to be knowledgeable about the broad content area so that she or he can take advantage of opportunities that arise to emphasize ideas that are particularly important. Additionally, the choice of ways to assess student work will similarly be guided by personal pedagogical knowledge of those obstacles that are commonly encountered by students in learning the particular science concepts.

Conclusion

This chapter has emphasized the indivisibility of teaching and assessment. In the classrooms of many teachers who integrate these aspects of classroom life, a culture of assessment is developed. In such classrooms, it is natural for teachers and students to talk continually about the quality of the work that is being done and the steps that might be taken to improve it. The ability to discuss the quality of one's own work, in fact, becomes a key goal of the course in itself, virtually indistinguishable from the science and how it is taught. In one such class (at the middle school level), the teacher conducts her parent conferences as a third party. That is, she remains silent when she meets with both parent and student. The student reports on his work, with specific examples of what he has done, what he has learned, and what he has yet to accomplish. The parent's questions are answered by his or her own child.

Reference

Bransford, J. D., Brown, A. L., and Cocking, R. R., eds. 1999. *How people learn: Brain, mind, experience, and school.* Washington, DC: National Academy Press.

Selected Bibliography

Black, P., and Wiliam, D. 1998. Inside the black box: Raising standards through classroom assessment. *Phi Delta Kappan* 80 (2): 139–48.

Hein, G., and Price. S. 1994. *Active assessment for active science.* Portsmouth, NH: Heinemann.

National Research Council (NRC). 1996. *National science education standards.* Washington, DC: National Academy Press (especially Chapters 3 and 5).

———. 2001. *Classroom assessment and the national science education standards.* Committee on Classroom Assessment and the *National Science Education Standards.* J. M. Atkin, P. Black, and J. Coffey, eds. Washington, DC: National Academy Press.

Sadler, R. 1989. Formative assessment and the design of instructional systems. *Instructional Science* 18: 119–44.

Wiggins, G. 1998. *Educative assessment.* San Francisco: Jossey-Bass.

Assessing Student Learning

Anne M. Cox-Petersen and Joanne K. Olson

Anne (Amy) Cox-Petersen is an assistant professor of education at California State University, Fullerton. She frequently teaches courses in educational foundations, elementary science methods, and graduate studies in elementary science education. As research associate at the Natural History Museum of Los Angeles County, she conducts visitor studies related to science learning. She is the author of numerous journal articles and conference presentations related to science teacher knowledge and informal science learning in museum and field settings. Her interest in assessment began as a classroom teacher in rural, suburban, and inner-city schools.

Joanne K. Olson is an assistant professor in the Center for Excellence in Science and Mathematics Education at Iowa State University. Before coming to Iowa State she taught science and elementary science methods to preservice teachers at the University of Southern California and California State University, Long Beach. Her interest in assessment began during her five years as a science teacher in inner-city and suburban Los Angeles and continues in her work with rural elementary schools across Iowa. She has authored several articles and given over sixty presentations regarding effective science teaching, and has received recognition at the local and national level for her teaching practice.

Learning science involves making connections and helping students link new information to their prior ideas and experiences. Assessing science learning allows students to demonstrate how they understand science concepts and make connections between concepts and skills and their lived experiences.

Many educators use *assessment* and *evaluation* to describe the same process even though the two terms differ in meaning. *Assessment* is an ongoing process that influences planning and implementing instruction. *Evaluation* refers to a cumulative event in which decisions are made in relation to students' grades for a reporting period or for a particular unit of study. Multiple assessment instruments and procedures are imperative when determining students' conceptual understanding of science and when making decisions about instruction. Moreover, effective science teachers assess more than conceptual understanding. They assess inquiry skills, work habits, and students' attitudes toward science and scientific processes.

Assessment has traditionally been viewed as a summative, end-of-unit indicator of how well students understand a topic. Research conducted over the last two decades on student learning in science indicates that assessment can serve a much broader purpose—to make students aware of their progress, to instill confidence to take on additional learning challenges, to promote metacognition and learning, and to be "a bridge to greater achievement, not a barrier to expanded opportunity" (Robinson 1996, 392).

How Do We Assess Student Learning in Science?

An important decision to be made before assessing student learning is where a teacher is taking his or her students. Teachers need to clearly articulate their goals for students, as well as the big science concepts students should be learning. Then, they should plan assessments directed toward those goals and concepts. One of our colleagues once lamented that we too often teach things we do not assess, and assess things we do not teach. One way to avoid this problem is to be clear on the desired outcomes in advance, then plan instruction and assessment toward that end. Many assessment strategies can be embedded within everyday instruction. One first-grade teacher who studied her own assessment practices reflected on her teaching as follows:

> *Assessment is best if embedded within instruction. Authentic assessment does not aim to assign a child a grade, but to determine what children know and where to go next.... I need to embed more assessment tools within the curriculum. I need to also consider a variety of assessment tools to make certain that I am actually assessing science knowledge and not another curriculum area such as writing. I need to choose tools that allow students comfort to reveal their knowledge of science.*

A problem with assessing student learning arises when there is a mismatch between the instructional strategies used by the teacher and the assessment techniques. For example, if students engage in cooperative group problem solving using hands-on materials, there would be discontinuity between the teaching strategy and assessment strategy if the teacher assessed student understanding with a multiple-choice written test. In this case, a written test would not allow students to show their problem-solving abilities and science process skills.

Summative and Formative Assessment

Summative assessments are typically administered following a unit of instruction to provide evidence about student understanding. Traditionally, students were tested primarily at the end of a unit of study and test scores were used to sort students or provide summative information about student achievement. Cognitive psychology research and studies of learning on educational practices have identified potential problems associated with end-of-unit assessment schemes. Students' test performance can be incongruent with their actual understanding of the concept. Many traditional tests, such as true/false, multiple choice, matching, and fill-in, do not indicate whether students understand something or whether they simply guessed correctly. Even open-ended tests can deceive teachers because students can become quite competent using scientific vocabulary, and answers may appear correct, even if the students do not know what the language means. Therefore, the teacher must consider assessment prompts very carefully.

To assess students' conceptual understanding, effective teachers constantly monitor students' thinking throughout instruction, not just at the end of a unit of study. This ongoing assessment is known as *formative assessment*. Like summative assessments, formative assessments are designed to help a teacher know what students are thinking and what sense they are making of the science they are studying. Decades of research on student thinking has indicated that what students put together is not always what teachers intended; learners often have elaborate "alternative" conceptions that are inconsistent with scientific ideas. Further, students' prior experiences, families, peers, and culture all influence what they learn. Critical to effective science instruction that results in robust understanding is a teacher who monitors what students think and probes that thinking, posing careful questions to challenge students' ideas and using that information to structure future questions, activities, and assessments. Classroom teachers can use the following guidelines to make sure that they are assessing their students throughout the entire instructional process.

1. *Find out what students know about the topic, then use that information to plan and guide instruction.*

Because students arrive in class with ideas of their own about the topic under study, it is critical for the teacher to find out what they know. Unfortunately, sometimes a teacher will collect this information—and then ignore it and teach the unit as planned. However, students' prior knowledge will affect what they learn, and information that doesn't seem to fit a student's prior understandings will most likely be ignored by him or her or simply be memorized with little conceptual understanding. Effective teaching requires that students' prior ideas be challenged with experiences and discussions and that students be given time to reflect and make sense of the new information. Unless a teacher knows students' prior ideas—and structures the experiences to confront them— those ideas may remain unchallenged and unchanged.

2. *Use formative assessment information to guide your teaching rather than grade your students.*

While some formative assessments may be graded, the primary purpose of formative assessment is to monitor student thinking in order to guide your teaching. This requires that the teacher carefully listen to students and ask probing questions to gain more information about their thinking. Formative assessment strategies are particularly useful when used throughout instruction to monitor student thinking and promote conceptual understanding.

Effective teachers focus on student understanding rather than the delivery of information. This shift toward a more student-centered classroom requires that the teacher be constantly alert to students' comments, questions, and ideas and take time to reflect on them. When teachers use a variety of strategies for formative assessment, a dual purpose is served. Formative assessments certainly help a teacher assess and monitor student thinking. But they also play an instructional role, helping students focus, attend to big concepts, monitor their own thinking, and think critically about what they are studying. These are processes the students are likely to go through only if the teacher provides time for reflection at the end of a lesson. This approach is far different from memorizing scientific vocabulary for a recall-based test, and requires that the teacher focus on basic science concepts and not view science as a set of isolated facts to be memorized.

3. *Engage in multidimensional assessment practices to gauge students' understanding and performance.*

Classroom teachers have many options when assessing student understanding before, during, and after instruction. A variety of assessment strategies exist and can be used for formative or summative purposes. Multiple assessment procedures during instruction can help a teacher better understand students' knowledge of science concepts and their demonstration of science skills. Nontraditional assessments show student knowledge in multiple ways and account for diverse learning styles, thereby providing more equitable assessment of students' knowledge and growth over time.

Assessment Strategies

The next section provides an overview of diverse assessment strategies that can provide feedback to students and teachers. By using multiple assessment practices, teachers can gauge student understanding over time and make important decisions about instruction.

Questioning

Perhaps the single most powerful tool in a teacher's repertoire is questioning. Effective teachers use their questions to elicit student *thinking*, not just to get the right answers. In addition, classroom dialogue enables students to articulate their ideas and listen to other viewpoints. The teacher's role during this time is to guide students toward understanding scientific concepts and to assist students in making connections between prior knowledge and new knowledge. This is also helpful because students can learn to identify and confront their own misconceptions. Compare the following two transcripts:

Teacher A: *April, what did you get when you looked at the loam sample?*

Student: *It came out clear.*

Teacher: *It came out clear. Good. Leticia, how much water did you get out of that?*

Student:	*About 0.5?*
Teacher:	*About half a milliliter. Right. You could hardly even measure that, could you?*

Teacher B:	*How would you describe the color of the lion in the picture?*
Student 1:	*Brownish-gray.*
Teacher:	*And why might that be so important?*
Student 1:	*Because it can blend in.*
Student 2:	*It will keep it from being eaten by something else.*
Student 3:	*Or maybe it will keep it from being seen by the animal it's trying to eat.*
Student 4:	*It's camouflaged.*
Teacher:	*And what do you mean by camouflage?*
Student 4:	*It's the same color so you can't see it very well.*

Teacher A obtains responses from students, but because they are short-answer questions that have a single right or wrong answer, the teacher gets short answers from students who seek the right answer. With so little information gained, the teacher has little choice but to ask another question. This type of questioning results in a large amount of time spent in "teacher talk" and short responses from students that indicate little of their thinking. Teacher B elicits multiple responses from students not only because of the open-ended nature of the second question, but because the teacher used wait time. Questioning alone is insufficient to get students talking. After you ask an effective question, wait three to five seconds before calling on someone, and most important, hold off on your response after a student answers. Teacher B avoided praising or repeating students' responses. Instead, the teacher looked at the students expectantly and eagerly, and the students continued to elaborate. When a student runs out of things to say, using wait time will encourage other students to add on. This gives the teacher more information about their thinking, and more time to develop a good follow-up question that builds on students' responses. Using wait time does not, however, guarantee good questions. Good teachers record the questions they intend to ask before class begins and use their questions to evoke high levels of thinking and analysis by their students.

Written Work
Pre-Instruction Assessment
In addition to critical teacher behaviors such as questioning, wait time, and responding, teachers can also have students complete a variety of written tasks to show their thinking. Because students' prior knowledge is such an important factor in their learning, having students draw or write their prior ideas is an effective strategy. Not only does this help the teacher understand student thinking so that appropriate instruction can be designed, but it helps students become more aware of their own ideas. The teacher can then have students refer back to their prior ideas and monitor how their own thinking is changing (or not changing!) in light of new experiences. In addition, students should be given the opportunity to explain why they are changing their ideas or holding onto their previous knowledge. This can be done at various points throughout a unit of study.

Reflective Journaling
Having students write brief journal entries into a science journal or learning log can be a convenient way for students to reflect on their own learning and for a teacher to monitor all students' thinking. Prompts can be general—"What was the big idea of today's lesson?" "Write about what you learned in class today"— or more specific— "How would this lab have been different if we had used calcium chloride instead of sodium chloride?" These tasks can be used to help students focus on the big idea or on connections between concepts or to direct them to specific learning objectives. Hanrahan (1999) recommends the use of journal writing as a tool to give English Language Learners (ELLs) practice in developing science language skills, thereby creating a more authentic environment for learning science.

Concept Maps
Concept maps are pictorial representations of concepts and how they fit together. Words or phrases are written within circles and connected by lines and labels to show how those ideas are linked. Concept maps typically have a hierarchical structure, with the most general idea somewhere near the middle of the map, and more specific concepts located further from the center. They can be used as a formative or summative assessment. Students can make concept maps at the beginning of the unit to show prior knowledge or they can develop them as the unit progresses, adding on to the map every two to three days or so. Students can create a concept map at the end of the unit as a formative assessment to show their overall understanding of a concept or concepts. Note the development shown between Concept Map #1 and Concept Map #2 on pages 112 and 113. They are both by the same student. Concept Map #1 was constructed in December; Concept Map #2 was constructed in the following spring after a unit on "Oceans." Teachers can assess student concept maps by counting the number of concepts, the number of links, the number of levels, and the sophistication and accuracy of the completed map. An example of a concept map

rubric that a teacher used to assess student knowledge about the ocean is presented in Table 1.

Table 1. Concept Map Rubric

5 points – Multiple connections between concepts. Includes specific names of nonliving structures, names of marine plants, microscopic organisms, and animals that are grouped according to scientific classification. Also includes one or more of the following: information about animal reproduction, behaviors, ancient sea life. Information is scientifically accurate.

4 points – Multiple connections between concepts. Includes at least three of the following with appropriate names: nonliving structures, plants, animals, microscopic organisms (plankton). Information is scientifically accurate.

3 points – Two or more connections between concepts. Includes at least two of the following: nonliving structures, plants, animals, microscopic organisms. Only one area that includes scientifically inaccurate information.

2 points – No connections between concepts. Includes at least two of the following: nonliving structures, plants, animals, microscopic organisms. Some scientifically inaccurate information.

1 point – No connections between concepts. Only one area of marine environments is included: nonliving structures, plants, animals. Some scientifically inaccurate information.

Maps can be created individually, in pairs, or groups, and the dialogue between students as they decide how the ideas fit together is usually quite rich and provides the teacher with a wealth of information. Novak (1990) has found that concept maps can be used to help students recognize and modify misconceptions. Using concept maps as a summative assessment tool requires that the task be specified, that a response format be clearly communicated to the students, and that a scoring system be developed prior to its use. Often, teachers and students will create scoring rubrics together. Nevertheless, concept mapping is a skill that requires practice. If using concept maps as a summative assessment, the teacher must be certain the students have had plenty of experience making concept maps.

Concept Map #1. Student A's concept map for the topic "Oceans" at the beginning of the unit.

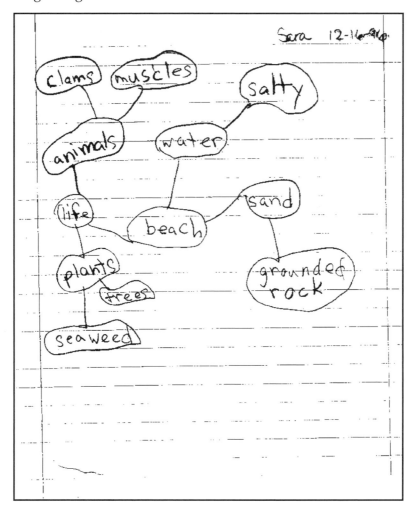

Concept Map #2. Student A's concept map for the topic "Oceans" at the end of the unit.

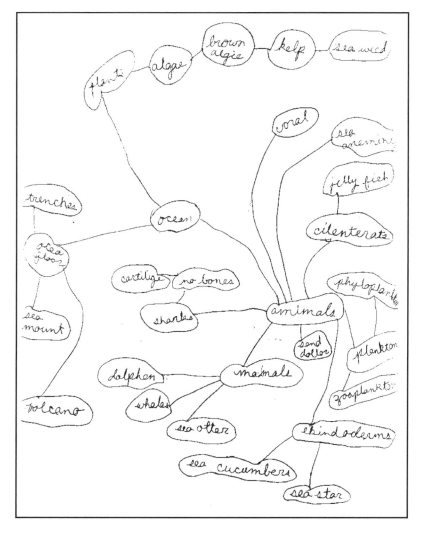

Written Tests

Traditional written tests are often problematic for English Language Learners because these students have a limited background to understand implicit meanings within the text of the test itself (Hafner and Ulanoff 1994). Further, many written tests assess only isolated facts unless great care is taken in creating the prompts. Creating a written test that requires students to convey their understandings of the science concepts is a difficult task. Open-ended assessments such as essay tests provide more information about students' understanding than closed-ended tests such as multiple-choice exams. However, even a multiple-choice question can be altered to require more thinking and elicit students' ideas. For example, rather than inventing incorrect responses for the other choices, students' misconceptions may be used as selections. In addition, students can be required to explain in one sentence why they chose the answer they did. While not ideal, because students can still guess an answer, modifying traditional assessments to better assess student thinking is a valuable strategy.

Observations

Good teachers are active observers, continuously gathering information about their students. Teachers can use checklists to determine science process skills their students are using or how they cooperate when working in small groups. Teachers can listen to student comments during small group work to determine how students are applying science concepts or dealing with misconceptions that arise. Checklists and anecdotal notes are helpful in recording specific information about observations made during class sessions. Anecdotal notes can be written on a label, then removed and placed by the student's name in a separate notebook. Checklists can be developed according to each unit of study and accompanying inquiry skills. Some teachers use technology to record observations more quickly and have them easily accessible for later use. Electronic personal organizers can be used to store class lists and checklists. Software can also be installed to accommodate digital camera photos.

Drawings

Student drawings often reveal more than do written responses. Words do not even have to be used, unless the student chooses to place some in the drawing. (See "before" and "after" drawings on page 115.) Drawings allow qualities of understanding to be revealed that may not be assessed by other means. They "bring out an affective component of understanding that most other probes leave untapped" (White and Gunstone 1992, 101). They may reveal misconceptions as well.

Scoring of drawings can be challenging. The drawing reveals a type of understanding that a student has, but not the sum total of it. Even developing a change score over time can problematic, because elements of a student's understanding may not be illustrated (Gunstone and White 1986). However, coupling drawings with other forms of assessment can help the teacher to better determine students' conceptual understanding. Furthermore, drawings do not require mastery of the English language and have fewer barriers than other assessment types for ELL students. Some teachers use a drawing coupled with a short interview, called a "draw and talk" technique. Students explain their drawings to the teacher, who can ask probing questions to gain more information.

Drawing #1. Student B's drawing of "The Ocean" in September.

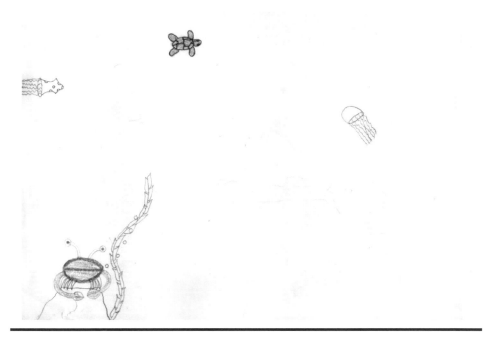

Drawing #2. Student B's drawing of "The Ocean" the following June.

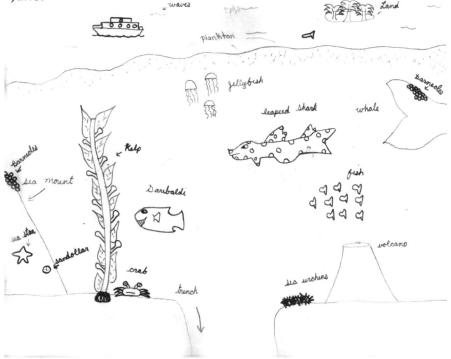

Performance and Portfolio Assessment

Performance assessment is considered by many educators and researchers as a more appropriate measure of student learning than traditional paper and pencil tests (e.g., Shavelson, Baxter, and Pine 1992; Stiggins 1994). With this type of assessment, students demonstrate their competence by performing or demonstrating a specific task. The level or quality of student performance can be increased when students prepare their work for an audience other than the teacher (Prain and Hand 1996). For example, a group of fifth-grade students investigated a local fish by observing the fish at an aquarium, communicating with marine biologists via e-mail, and using a variety of reference materials. To show their understanding, they created a slide show using PowerPoint and presented it to family and friends at a science conference.

A portfolio can include student performances or exhibitions, such as the PowerPoint slide show, as well as other work samples that help demonstrate students' mastery of specific concepts or skills. Bloom (1998) describes two different types of portfolios: (a) those that are developed personally with a collection of student work and (b) those that are a focused collection of evidence that students organize to support a particular knowledge claim. In either case, students make the final decision about what should be included and write reflections about their work indicating why it was included within their portfolio.

Interviews

Individual or small-group interviews provide in-depth information about students' understanding of science and misconceptions that they may have. Interviews can be used formatively or summatively and can gauge students' understanding many months after a concept was studied. Interviews can consist of teacher-developed questions or they can focus on students' explanations of their work. Interviews require students to explain their thinking while teachers use them to probe for additional information. Teachers can informally interview students as they are working at their desks or set aside a specific time to interview students individually.

Self-Evaluation and Attitude Surveys

Students can be active participants in assessing their understanding of science, their scientific skills, and their attitude toward learning science. Students can record their prior knowledge at the beginning of the unit and then return to this information and monitor how their ideas are changing, what is causing their ideas to change, and what further information they think they need. This process provides focus for their learning and can be done with concept maps, journal prompts, KWL charts (What do we Know? What do we Want to know, What have we Learned?), and so on.

Attitude assessments can be used throughout the school year to gauge students' interest in a variety of content and activities. Usually, attitude surveys are paper and pencil scales that require multiple-choice answers. Primary grade teachers often use pictures of a range of faces—from very happy to very sad—to gauge their students' opinions. However, students can draw their feelings or write about them in their science journals as well.

Scoring Students' Work

Scoring

Numeric scoring is often required by the public to provide mathematical data as an indicator of student achievement. However, all students benefit from feedback that is more than a number. In order for students to evaluate their performance and understanding, appropriate feedback is critical. Feedback should be specific and designed to help the student gain a greater understanding of the concepts being studied. For example, "You should be pleased about the link you made between the role of the herbivores in this habitat and the limited species of plants. The next step will be to consider how the predators will have an impact on this habitat over time." In this example, the comment is directed toward the student ("You should be pleased" rather than "I like the way you..."). While subtle, it shifts the focus away from pleasing the teacher. The comment also directly addresses an area of strength, and the next area for the student to consider.

Rubrics

Rubrics can be used to determine criteria and expectations for various science assignments. They can be used in conjunction with student interviews, drawings, science journals, and other artifacts.

Fourth- and fifth-grade students were asked to "draw a picture of what is in the ocean, using as much detail as possible." The following is an example of a rubric that was used to determine their conceptual understanding.

0 points = No drawing or a drawing of one organism and the water surface

1 point = Two or more animals, water surface

2 points = Plants or the ocean floor, two or more animals

3 points = Swimming and stationary animals, plants and ocean floor

4 points = Ocean floor with features, swimming and stationary animals, plants, most are accurately placed

5 points = Extensive ocean floor features with appropriate organisms, many animals and plants, accurate placement, shows some relationships between organisms (e.g., a baleen whale eating krill)

While rubrics are a useful device for teachers to ensure consistent scoring, we recommend that teachers provide a rubric in advance of the assignment or have students help create the rubric. This helps teachers and students define expected performance and standards.

Conclusion

We propose that science teachers use ongoing assessment throughout the school year, in a variety of forms. Assessment should be aligned with learning goals and instructional strategies, not viewed as separate from what and how students are learning. Moreover, teachers should plan for assessment in the context of students' lives and experiences and assessments should be inclusive of all students.

As the literature continues to expand regarding the use of concept maps, drawings, presentations, and other forms of alternative assessment, we hope that teachers and science educators will become more knowledgeable about how they can best be used in the science classroom. While we strongly believe that every student should develop literacy skills, assessing conceptual understanding in science using only traditional assessments misrepresents students' understanding and can be especially problematic for English Language Learners. Instead, we advocate that alternative forms of assessment be used in addition to written tests. This view is consistent with the *National Science Education Standards* (NRC 1996), which encourage teachers to "use multiple methods and systematically gather data about student understanding and ability" (37). Further, "each mode of assessment serves particular purposes and particular students. Each has particular strengths and weaknesses and is used to gather different kinds of information about student understanding and ability" (38). As schools become increasingly diverse, science teachers and science teacher educators need to determine ways to teach *and* assess science effectively.

References

Bloom, J. W. 1998. *Creating a classroom community of young scientists.* Toronto: Irwin.

Gunstone, R. F., and White, R. T. 1986. Assessing understanding by means of Venn diagrams. *Science Education* 70: 151–58.

Hafner, A. L., and Ulanoff, S. H. 1994. Validity issues and concerns for assessing English learners. *Education and Urban Society* 26: 367–89.

Hanrahan, M. 1999. Rethinking science literacy: Enhancing communication and participation in school science through affirmational dialogue journal writing. *Journal of Research in Science Teaching* 36: 699–717.

National Research Council (NRC). 1996. *National science education standards.* Washington, DC: National Academy Press.

Novak, J. D. 1990. Concept mapping: A useful tool for science education. *Journal of Research in Science Teaching* 27: 937–49.

Prain, V., and Hand, B. 1996. Writing for learning in secondary science: Rethinking practices. *Teaching and Teacher Education* 12: 609–26.

Robinson, S. P. 1996. With numeracy for all: Urban schools and the reform of mathematics education. *Urban Education* 30: 379–94.

Shavelson, R. J., Baxter, G. P., and Pine, J. 1992. Performance assessments: Political rhetoric and measurement reality. *Educational Researcher* 21: 22–27.

Stiggins, R. 1994. *Student-centered classroom assessment.* New York: Macmillan.

White, R., and Gunstone, R. 1992. *Probing understanding.* London, England: Falmer Press.

PART 5

Professional Development and the Science of Learning

Curriculum Reform, Professional Development, and Powerful Learning

Janet Carlson Powell, James B. Short, and Nancy M. Landes

Janet Carlson Powell is the associate director at the BSCS (Biological Science Curriculum Study) in Colorado Springs. In this capacity, she oversees the curriculum development, professional development, and research divisions of the organization. She has been active in science education for more than 20 years with a range of experiences including teaching middle school and high school life and earth science, teaching science methods for preservice and master teachers, developing university-school partnerships to improve science teaching and learning, developing innovative science curriculum materials, leading professional development activities in science education, and conducting school-based research.

James B. Short is the project director of the SCI (Science Curriculum Implementation) Center at BSCS (Biological Science Curriculum Study). Funded by the National Science Foundation, the SCI Center assists high school and district leadership teams with selecting and implementing standards-based curriculum materials. Prior to BSCS, he was the director of science education for Edison Schools, Inc. He has ten years experience teaching high school biology using BSCS curriculum materials. In 1998 he was the recipient of the BSCS Teacher of the Year Award.

Nancy M. Landes is a senior science educator at BSCS (Biological Science Curriculum Study) where she has directed both curriculum development and professional development projects. Currently director of the Professional Development Division at BSCS, she began her professional career as a classroom teacher in grades four and five and joined the BSCS staff in 1983. She leads a cooperative professional development project with the National Science Teachers Association to extend the efforts of the "Building a Presence" project. She is particularly interested in helping teachers make the connections between curriculum implementation, professional development, and student learning and in establishing the conditions that make possible the successful implementation of meaningful instructional strategies in science classrooms.

Teachers are key to enhancing learning in schools. In order to teach in a manner consistent with new theories of learning, extensive learning opportunities for teachers are required. We assume that what is known about learning applies to teachers as well as students. Yet teacher learning is a relatively new topic of research, so there is not a great deal of data about it. Nevertheless, there are a number of rich case studies that investigate teachers' learning over extended time periods and these cases, plus other information, provide data on learning opportunities available to teachers from the perspective of what is known about how people learn. (Bransford, Brown, and Cocking 1999, 191–92)

Educators have long been interested in the translation of theory into practice. The research on learning as synthesized in *How People Learn: Brain, Mind Experience, and School* (hereafter referred to as *HPL*) (Bransford, Brown, and Cocking 1999) provides a wonderful opportunity for considering how educators can translate what is known about learning into actual classroom practice that results in powerful learning for both teachers and students. In this chapter, we will consider the roles of curriculum implementation and professional development in promoting powerful learning.

We argue that curriculum reform is an essential component in improving the learning and teaching of science. Curriculum reform is a systemic approach to changing *what* we are teaching in science as well as *how* we teach it. One way to participate in curriculum reform is to adopt materials that are standards-based in their approach to content, assessment, teaching, and professional development. Such materials have the greatest potential for influencing teacher and student learning. Standards-based materials have the following elements: they include inquiry as a part of the science content; the instructional strategies and design encourage a constructivist approach to learning; and sustainable implementation of the materials requires ongoing professional development. The professional development that supports the implementation of standards-based curriculum materials requires a transformation in teachers' ideas about and understanding of subject matter, teaching, and the learning of science.

To consider the important relationship between standards-based curriculum implementation and professional development, we begin by looking at the key findings from *HPL* in terms of student learning. Then we proceed to an understanding of how curriculum materials can embody these findings. Because the result is nontraditional curriculum materials, we then consider the role of professional development for increasing the effectiveness of those materials. Finally, we weave the individual pieces together with an illustration of a professional development strategy that begins with selecting materials for curriculum reform.

How People Learn and Curriculum Reform

In *HPL*, the authors summarize three key findings about learning, based on an exhaustive study of the research. The following statements capture the essence of these findings:

1. Students come to the classroom with preconceptions about how the world works. These preconceptions shape how new learning is assimilated.

2. To develop competence in an area of inquiry, students must have a deep foundation of knowledge, have an understanding of how this knowledge relates to a framework, and be able to organize that knowledge so that it can be retrieved and applied.

3. Students must be taught explicitly to take control of their own learning by defining goals and monitoring their progress toward meeting those goals.

These findings about student learning have parallel implications for science teaching, which then suggest a translation of those implications into curriculum materials. As the authors of *HPL* note (in pages 19–21), the findings imply that science teachers must be able to do the following:

◆ Recognize and draw out preconceptions from their students and base instructional decisions on the information they get from their students.

In other words, for students to learn science effectively, we need to teach from a perspective that recognizes the knowledge students walk into the classroom with every day and use this knowledge and experience as the base for building new concepts.

◆ Teach their subject matter in depth so that facts are conveyed in a context with examples and within a conceptual framework.

We must help students build a rich foundation about science. This is accomplished by considering science content not as isolated pieces of information, but as a set of larger concepts with associated facts that illustrate the concepts. Implicit in this recommendation is the idea that we must help students understand the framework of each scientific discipline they study.

◆ Integrate metacognitive skills into the curriculum and teach those skills explicitly.

We must be direct in our science teaching about "how to learn." Students do not automatically know how to set reasonable goals for learning, connect ideas together so their learning is meaningful, or be reflective about their own progress.

Competent science teachers who know their subject matter well and have a strong grasp of the pedagogical content knowledge that is needed to effectively teach that subject matter well can accomplish the type of teaching implied in *HPL*. Pedagogical content knowledge is the information that enables a teacher to teach a particular subject area in an appropriate manner. This includes knowing which ideas build on each other and what prior conceptions students might bring to the classroom (Shulman 1986). The task of identifying prior concepts and building on them can be simplified, however, if the curriculum materials available for teaching science incorporate these essential ideas in a manner appropriate to instructional materials. It is clear from the analysis of curriculum and instruction in the TIMSS project (Schmidt et al. 1999) and the work of AAAS (in press) that these ideas for instruction are not commonly practiced in U.S. classrooms or well supported in the most widely used instructional materials. Nevertheless, we believe it is possible to make connections from the research about learning to specific means of instruction and science curriculum materials. Table 1 provides an overview of how the key findings from *HPL* might be explicitly addressed in curriculum materials.

Table 1. Relating the Key Findings from *How People Learn: Brain, Mind, Experience, and School* to Curriculum Materials

Key Findings: Students	Key Findings: Teachers	As a Result, Materials Need to
1. Come to class with preconceptions	Recognize preconceptions and adjust instruction	◆ Include structured strategies to elicit and challenge student preconceptions ◆ Incorporate background for the teacher about common preconceptions
2. Need to develop a deep factual understanding based in a conceptual framework	Understand the content and conceptual framework for a discipline Provide examples for context	◆ Be organized around a conceptual framework ◆ Connect factual information to the framework ◆ Provide relevant examples to illustrate key ideas
3. Set goals and analyze progress toward them	Provide class time for goal setting and analysis Teach metacognitive skills	◆ Make learning goals explicit ◆ Integrate metacognitive skill development into content

An Example of Curriculum Materials That Are Designed to Increase Student Learning

We have chosen to highlight *BSCS Biology: A Human Approach* (BSCS 1997) (henceforth referred to as *BB: AHA*) as an example of a curricular program that exemplifies many of the ideas listed in Table 1. This program was ranked highly in a recent review of biology textbooks (Morse et al. 2001). In particular, the reviewers noted that "this book is clearly linked to NSES (*National Science Education Standards*), not only in the content, but also in the pedagogy, professional development and implementation suggestions" (16). Three key features of *BB: AHA* highlight aspects of curriculum materials that could increase student learning if implemented well. First, the materials are used as an instructional model that helps teachers access students' prior knowledge. Second, the materials are organized around six unifying themes of biology, rather than isolated facts and biological topics. Third, students are active participants in the assessment of their own learning. Each of these features provides an opportunity for teachers to increase student learning, even though the resulting materials may look different from what teachers are used to seeing. We discuss each feature below to show just how the curriculum materials are different.

Table 2. Summary of the BSCS 5E Instructional Model as Used in *BSCS Biology: A Human Approach*

Phase	Summary
Engage	The instructor assesses the learners' prior knowledge and helps them become engaged in a new concept by reading a vignette, posing questions, doing a demonstration that has a nonintuitive result (a discrepant event), showing a video clip, or conducting some other short activity that promotes curiosity and elicits prior knowledge.
Explore	Learners work in collaborative teams to complete lab activities that help them use prior knowledge to generate ideas, explore questions and possibilities, and design and conduct a preliminary inquiry.
Explain	To explain their understanding of the concept, learners may make presentations, share ideas with one another, review current scientific explanations and compare these to their own understanding, and/or listen to an explanation from the teacher that guides the learners toward a more in-depth understanding.
Elaborate	Learners elaborate their understanding of the concept by conducting additional lab activities. They may revisit an earlier lab and build on it, or conduct an activity that requires an application of the concept.
Evaluate	The evaluation phase helps both learners and instructors assess how well the learners understand the concept and whether they have met the learning outcomes.

Feature 1: An Instructional Model

To help learners understand key concepts and meet the designated outcomes, BSCS develops curriculum materials and designs professional development using an instructional model based on a constructivist theory of learning, known throughout the educational community as the "BSCS 5E Instructional Model." The 5Es are *engage, explore, explain, elaborate,* and *evaluate* and are described in Table 2. In *BB: AHA,* each chapter is organized using the 5Es. Students begin their study of a biological concept by articulating what they know already (or think they know), and then they explore the concept further through experimentation. Next, the teacher introduces the currently accepted scientific explanation in the context of the students' explorations. This 5E sequence of exploring before explaining may be the most unfamiliar aspect to teachers because it feels like they are "holding back" information. In reality, this sequence provides students an opportunity to place new knowledge in the context of what they already know and therefore addresses key findings 1 and 2 from *HPL* (see Table 1).

Feature 2: Conceptual Organization

The second feature of *BB: AHA* that is different from most biology textbooks is the organization of the content. The six units of the program are based on six unifying principles of science. These principles form the framework for each unit and the content connects back to the big idea within a context that makes sense to the learner. See Table 3 for a list of the units and the chapter titles within each unit for an illustration of how a biology program can be organized conceptually. This feature is one way curriculum materials can attend to the second key finding from *HPL*, but is not necessarily a familiar approach for teachers who may have learned biology from a topical or taxonomic approach.

Table 3. Units and Chapters in *BSCS Biology: A Human Approach*

Units	Chapters
Evolution: Patterns and Products of Change in Living Systems	◆ The Human Animal ◆ Evolution: Change Across Time ◆ Products of Evolution: Unity and Diversity
Homeostasis: Maintaining Dynamic Equilibrium in Living Systems	◆ The Internal Environment of Organisms ◆ Maintaining Balance in Organisms ◆ Human Homeostasis: Health and Disease
Energy, Matter, and Organization: Relationships in Living Systems	◆ Performance and Fitness ◆ The Cellular Basis of Activity ◆ The Cycling of Matter and the Flow of Energy in Communities
Continuity: Reproduction and Inheritance in Living Systems	◆ Reproduction in Humans and Other Organisms ◆ Continuity of Information through Inheritance ◆ Gene Action
Development: Growth and Differentiation in Living Systems	◆ Processes and Patterns of Development ◆ The Human Life Span
Ecology: Interaction and Interdependence in Living Systems	◆ Interdependence among Organisms in the Biosphere ◆ Decision Making in a Complex World

Feature 3: Metacognitive Skills

One way in which students' metacognitive skills are developed in *BB: AHA* is student involvement with their own assessment. The fifth "E" in the 5E instructional model is *evaluate*. During this phase of the instructional model, both the teacher and the student are responsible for assessing the student's understanding. Students do this by identifying what they have learned and how they learned. This level of reflection helps increase students' awareness and understanding of the learning process. This direct student involvement is not common in U.S. schools and involves using a set of strategies that may be unfamiliar to the teacher or not supported by the administration.

These three features of *BB: AHA*, along with the several other unique characteristics, help explain why in curriculum reform professional development must be ongoing. In fact, professional development needs to start with the selection of curriculum materials, not the use of them. In the next section, we describe a model of professional development in the context of curriculum reform, including a specific example focused on the selection of standards-based curriculum materials.

The Case for Professional Development When Implementing Standards-Based Curriculum Materials

As indicated in the example above, the implementation of standards-based curriculum materials may be a significant change for teachers in their approach to learning and teaching science. Because curricula such as *BB: AHA* and others (see Table 4 or visit the SCI Center website: *www.scicenteratbscs.org*) require conceptual understanding of science content, knowledge of the research on how students learn, and pedagogical content knowledge to be effectively used, comprehensive professional development aimed at improving instruction and learning is important. Highly structured, standards-based curriculum materials, when combined with effective, sustained professional development, have the potential for changing science teaching practices in a manner that can lead to improved student achievement and attitudes. For this potential to emerge, professional development interventions need to incorporate multiple elements of instruction—the teachers, students, content, and environments—and the interactions among these elements (Cohen and Ball 2001).

Characteristics of Effective Professional Development

The *National Science Education Standards* (NRC 1996) state that professional development for teachers of science requires opportunities to learn science content through the perspectives and methods of inquiry; to learn how to teach science in a way that integrates knowledge of science, learning, pedagogy, and students; and to build an understanding and ability for lifelong learning. Also, professional development programs for teachers of science must be coherent and integrated. The National Institute for Science Education (Loucks-Horsley, Stiles, and Hewson 1996) synthesized a variety of professional development standards to produce a list of principles of effective professional development experiences for science educators:

◆ They are driven by a clear, well-defined image of effective classroom learning and teaching.

◆ They provide teachers with opportunities to develop knowledge and skills and broaden their teaching approaches, so they can create better learning opportunities for students.

Table 4. Standards-Based Science Instructional Materials

Discipline	Instructional Materials	Grade Level	Developer	Publisher
Earth Science	Earth System Science in the Community (EarthComm)	9–12	American Geological Institute	It's About Time Publishing
Physical Science	Active Physics	9–12	Arthur Eisenkraft	It's About Time Publishing
	Chem Discovery	10–12	University of Northern Colorado	Kendall/Hunt Publishing Co.
	Chemistry in the Community (ChemCom)	9–12	American Chemical Society	W.H. Freeman and Co.
	Comprehensive Conceptual Curriculum for Physics (C³P)	9–10	University of Dallas Physics Department	University of Dallas Physics Department
	Hands-On Physics	11–12	Concord Consortium	Concord Consortium
	Introductory Physical Science (IPS)	9	Science Curriculum, Inc.	Science Curriculum, Inc.
	Minds-On Physics	11–12	University of Massachusetts Physics Ed. Research Group	Kendall/Hunt Publishing Co.
Life Science	Biology: A Community Context	9–12	William Leonard John Penick	Glencoe/McGraw-Hill
	BSCS Biology: A Human Approach	9–11	Biological Sciences Curriculum Study	Kendall/Hunt Publishing Co.
	BSCS Biology: A Molecular Approach (Blue Version)	10–11	Biological Sciences Curriculum Study	Glencoe/McGraw-Hill
	BSCS Biology: An Ecological Approach (Green Version)	9–11	Biological Sciences Curriculum Study	Kendall/Hunt Publishing Co.
	Insights in Biology	9–10	Education Development Center	Kendall/Hunt Publishing Co.
Integrated Science	Ecology: A Systems Approach	9–12	TERC	Kendall/Hunt Publishing Co.
	Global Lab	9	TERC	Kendall/Hunt Publishing Co.
	Prime Science	9–10	University of California Berkeley	Kendall/Hunt Publishing Co.
	Science in a Technical World	9–12	American Chemical Society	W.H. Freeman and Co.
	SEPUP: Issues, Evidence & You	9	Lawrence Hall of Science	Lab-Aids, Inc.
	SEPUP: Science and Sustainability	10–12	Lawrence Hall of Science	Lab-Aids, Inc.

◆ They use instructional methods to promote learning for adults, which mirror the methods to be used with students.

◆ They build or strengthen the learning community of science teachers.

◆ They prepare and support teachers to serve in leadership roles that require them to step beyond their classrooms and play roles in the development of the whole school and beyond.

◆ They consciously provide links to the other parts of the educational system.

◆ They include continuous assessment.

While professional development experiences designed to support the implementation of new curriculum materials need to incorporate all of these principles, we have chosen to focus on the third principle. Curriculum materials designed to increase student learning, such as *BB: AHA*, convey a view of teaching largely as a process of provoking students to think about and conduct scientific inquiries, supporting students as they work, and guiding them along productive paths to reach the intended learning outcomes. How are teachers who are unaccustomed to this approach to learning and teaching going to learn the strategies and pedagogical content knowledge necessary to effectively implement curriculum materials that have these goals? We suggest that professional development experiences for teachers model the instructional approach intended with students by becoming the strategy for how teachers learn to implement the new curriculum materials. In other words, professional development that is a powerful learning experience for teachers should be designed so it incorporates the same elements that provide powerful learning for students.

Standards-based curriculum materials challenge teachers to think differently about learning and teaching science. Instead of a textbook that provides only "what to teach," these curriculum materials also provide instructional support for "how to teach." Because incorporating this type of support into curriculum materials makes the materials different, most teachers need a rich form of ongoing professional development to help them learn how to use such materials effectively. For these experiences to model the instructional approaches used in the curriculum materials themselves, professional development needs to be a powerful learning experience for teachers. Our contention is that professional development that supports the implementation of standards-based curriculum materials must challenge teachers' current beliefs about learning and teaching science. In other words, the professional development to learn how to use reform-based curricula needs to transform—change the nature of—teachers' beliefs and practices. Five features that characterize transformative professional development (Thompson and Zeuli 1999) are as follows:

◆ Create a sufficiently high level of cognitive dissonance to disturb in some fundamental way the equilibrium between teachers' existing beliefs and practices on the one hand and their experience with subject matter, students' learning, and teaching on the other.

◆ Provide time, contexts, and support for teachers to think—to work at resolving the dissonance through discussion, reading, writing, and other activities that essentially amount to the crystallization, externalization, criticism, and revision of their thinking.

◆ Ensure that the dissonance-creating and dissonance-resolving activities are connected to the teacher's own students and context, or something similar.

◆ Provide a way for teachers to develop a repertoire for practice that is consistent with the new understandings that teachers are building.

◆ Provide continuing help in the cycle of (1) surfacing the new issues and problems that will inevitably arise from actual classroom performance, (2) deriving new understandings from them, (3) translating these new understandings into performance, and (4) recycling.

These characteristics of transformative professional development are related to the constructivist philosophy of teaching and learning on which the BSCS 5E Instructional Model is based and are consistent with the key findings about learning and teaching from *HPL*. In other words, powerful learning for adults parallels powerful learning for students.

Using the Selection of Curriculum Materials as a Professional Development Strategy

Curriculum implementation can be an effective professional development strategy (Loucks-Horsley et al. 1998). This strategy provides teachers with ways to learn about, experiment with, reflect on, and share information about learning and teaching in the context of implementing new curriculum materials with colleagues. Consequently, teachers strengthen their content and pedagogical knowledge and skills as they implement the new curriculum. This strategy is most effective, of course, when the curriculum materials being implemented are standards-based and exemplify the recent research on learning and teaching.

When teachers review materials during a curriculum review process, standards-based curriculum materials often stand apart from more traditional curricula because they are not organized or formatted in the usual way. Often, standards-based materials do not get a positive reception because they are misunderstood. Consequently, the process of *selection and adoption* of curriculum materials should be considered a professional development opportunity. As such, it deserves a process that exemplifies effective practices of transformative professional development, such as the Analyzing Instructional Materials (AIM) Process used by the SCI Center at BSCS.

The SCI (Science Curriculum Implementation) Center at BSCS is a high school implementation center funded by the National Science Foundation. The mission of the SCI Center at BSCS is to assist school- and district-based teams as they build the leadership capacity to implement an effective science education program using reform-oriented, standards-based curriculum materials. The National Academy for Curriculum Leadership (NACL) is the cornerstone of the SCI Center's work. The NACL is a three-year professional development experience for leadership teams to learn how to select curriculum materials, design professional development for the implementation of those materials, and develop strategies to determine the impact of the materials on student learning and teaching practice. To help schools and districts make better decisions about the selection and adoption of reform-oriented curriculum materials, the SCI Center staff is using the AIM Process, a procedure for analyzing instructional materials. The AIM Process was developed collaboratively as a joint project between the SCI Center at BSCS and the K–12 Alliance, a division of WestEd.

The AIM Process is an evidence-based process for analyzing curriculum materials and was designed as a professional development experience to support curriculum implementation. Using an inquiry-based approach that is consistent with a constructivist view of learning, the AIM Process focuses on asking questions, gathering information, and making decisions about curriculum materials based on evidence. Rather than allowing teachers to take a cursory glance at the science content covered in a textbook, the AIM Process encourages teachers to think about the importance of curriculum materials to the learning process for students and to the instructional process for teachers. During the AIM Process, teachers and administrators, working as a team, first complete a graphic organizer of the conceptual flow of the content from a unit of instruction. They then analyze evidence from the curriculum materials related to the science content, the work students do, the work teachers do, and how student learning is assessed. After they complete this detailed screening process that leads to a decision, the selected curriculum materials are piloted so that teachers and administrators can design more effective professional development for curriculum implementation. As a result, piloting and designing professional development are informed by what is learned about the curriculum materials themselves from the AIM Process.

In this chapter, our focus is on curriculum materials that support how students learn science, so we will showcase how teachers use the AIM Process to examine the work students do. After teachers use the AIM Process to develop a graphic organizer of the content from an instructional unit (see Figure 1 for an example), they complete three steps to analyze the nature and depth of the work students do. In the first step, they review the rubric for "The Work Students Do" (see Table 5). The rubric has four components: the quality of the learning experiences, the fundamental understandings about scientific inquiry, the abilities necessary to do scientific inquiry, and the accessibility of the curriculum materials. Next, they return to the unit of instruction under review and gather evidence about the types of activities students do and the work students produce. They think about the question: How does an activity help students develop an understanding of the science concept presented? During the third and final step, teachers use their evidence of activities that promote student learning to score the components on the rubric.

Figure 1. An Example of a Graphic Organizer from the AIM Process Showing How Teachers Might Illustrate the Connections among Major Concepts in a Unit from *BSCS Biology: A Human Approach.*

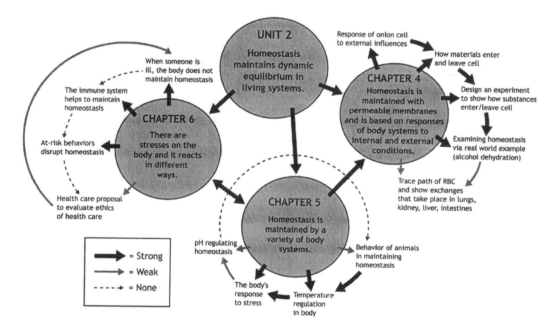

The AIM Process challenges teachers and science administrators to develop some common understandings about the curriculum materials under review. Most teachers come to the process of selecting materials with the goal of finding a textbook that contains the science content required by their district or state standards. Although content alignment is important, it is not the only selection criterion a teacher or administrator should use to select curriculum materials, especially those materials that were designed to address how students learn science. As a result of completing the AIM Process, teachers gain insights into the continuity and depth of reform-oriented curriculum materials and a better understanding of standards-based approaches to learning and teaching science. Throughout the process, participants usually experience some form of dissonance about how curriculum materials can provide guidance for not only *what* to teach, but *how* to teach science concepts in ways that address how students learn. The process provides multiple opportunities for teachers

Table 5. Rubric for Use during the Analyzing Instructional Materials (AIM) Process

"Work Students Do" Rubric	When using these curriculum materials . . .		
	(5 points)	**(3 points)**	**(1 point)**
Quality Learning Experiences Quality learning experiences have these features: ◆ Learning goals are clearly defined within an inquiry-based learning cycle/sequence. ◆ Activities are engaging, relevant, and developmentally appropriate for students. ◆ Students control their own learning by monitoring their progress in achieving learning goals. ◆ Student collaboration is an integral part of the learning experience. ◆ Students use a variety of resources (e.g., equipment, media, technology) in and out of the classroom to explore ideas and solve problems.	Students engage in quality learning experiences that lead to increased understanding of key science concepts.	Students engage in activities that have some of the characteristics of quality learning experiences.	Students engage in activities that have few of the characteristics of quality learning experiences.
Abilities Necessary to Do Scientific Inquiry Students doing scientific inquiry involves ◆ Asking and identifying questions and concepts to guide scientific investigations ◆ Designing and conducting scientific investigations ◆ Using appropriate technology and mathematics to enhance investigations ◆ Formulating and revising explanations and models ◆ Analyzing alternative explanations and models	Students engage in investigations that are integral to their conceptual understanding of science. Investigations provide students the opportunity to use scientific inquiry and develop abilities to think and act in ways associated with inquiry.	Students participate in investigations that partially contribute to the student's understanding of key science concepts. Investigations provide experiences that focus on some of the fundamental abilities of scientific inquiry.	Students participate in few, if any, meaningful investigations. Opportunities to develop the abilities necessary to do scientific inquiry are limited or absent.

Table 5 Continues on following page

Table 5 Continued from preceding page

"Work Students Do" Rubric	When using these curriculum materials . . .		
	(5 points)	(3 points)	(1 point)
Fundamental Understandings about Scientific Inquiry The work scientists do includes ◆ Inquiring about how physical, living, or designed systems function ◆ Conducting investigations for a variety of reasons ◆ Utilizing a variety of tools, technology, and methods to enhance their investigations ◆ Utilizing mathematical tools and models to improve all aspects of investigations ◆ Proposing explanations based on evidence, logic, and historical and current scientific knowledge ◆ Communicating and collaborating with other scientists in ways that are clear, accurate, logical, and open to questioning ◆ Accurately and effectively communicating results and responding appropriately to critical comments ◆ Generating additional testable questions	Students engage in meaningful and integral experiences to increase their understanding of how scientists work and what they do. Students make connections between their own work and the work scientists do.	Students engage in experiences to partially increase their understanding of how scientists work and what they do. Students make occasional connections between their own work and the work scientists do.	Students engage in few, if any, experiences to increase their understanding of how scientists work and what they do. Students rarely make connections between their own work and the work scientists do.
Accessibility When addressing the diversity of learners, consider the following: ◆ Varied learning abilities/disabilities ◆ Special needs (e.g., auditory, visual, physical, speech, emotional) ◆ English language proficiency ◆ Cultural differences ◆ Different learning styles ◆ Gender	The work students do is consistently accessible to diverse learners, providing opportunities for all students to achieve.	The work students do is often accessible to diverse learners, providing some opportunities for all students to achieve.	The work students do lacks accessibility to diverse learners, providing limited opportunities for all students to achieve.

and administrators to work collaboratively to resolve this dissonance through reading, discussion, reflection, and working with a trained facilitator of the process. In the end, science teachers and administrators construct a shared understanding of how well specific curriculum materials meet the needs of their students and in the process develop some abilities for gathering evidence to support their decisions. In this way, the AIM Process becomes a transformative professional development experience because participants often change their beliefs about the nature of science, teaching, and learning through a directed, constructivist approach to curriculum selection and adoption.

Conclusion

We began this chapter by stating that curriculum reform is a systemic matter requiring the implementation of standards-based curriculum materials and transformative professional development. This combination can result in radical changes in teachers' ideas about and understanding of subject matter, teaching, and the learning of science. Through curriculum implementation and its companion, professional development, more students ultimately will learn more science effectively. Until the pedagogy of professional development for curriculum implementation becomes transformative, however, the long-term impact of standards-based curricula will fall short of its potential to support sustainable reform.

To reach the goal of systemic curriculum reform, science teachers should keep the following in mind:

◆ We know something about powerful learning and this information can be used to develop effective curriculum materials and to design equally powerful professional development experiences.

◆ Curriculum reform includes the implementation of standards-based instructional materials and ongoing professional development.

◆ Standards-based curriculum materials address standards not only for content, but also for teaching and professional development.

◆ Teachers will better understand standards-based materials when they experience ongoing professional development that begins with thinking about the selection of materials in a new and more meaningful way.

◆ The combination of effective curriculum implementation and transformative professional development yields powerful learning for all.

References

American Association for the Advancement of Science (AAAS). (In press). *Resources for science literacy: Curriculum materials evaluation.* New York: Oxford University Press.

Bransford, J. D., Brown, A. L., and Cocking, R. R., eds. 1999. *How people learn: Brain, mind, experience, and school.* Washington, D.C.: National Academy Press.

BSCS. 1993. *Developing biological literacy: A guide to developing secondary and post-secondary biology curricula.* Dubuque, IA: Kendall/Hunt.

———. 1997. *BSCS biology: A human approach.* Dubuque, IA: Kendall/Hunt.

Cohen, D. K., and Ball, D. L. 2001. Making change: Instruction and its improvement. *Phi Delta Kappan* 83(1): 73–77.

Loucks-Horsley, S., Hewson, P., Love, N., and Stiles, K. 1998. *Designing professional development for teachers of science and mathematics.* Thousand Oaks, CA: Corwin Press.

Loucks-Horsley, S., Stiles, K., and Hewson, P. 1996. *Principles of effective professional development for mathematics and science education: A synthesis of standards.* Madison: University of Wisconsin at Madison, National Institute for Science Education.

Morse, M. P., and the AIBS Review Team. 2001. *A review of biological instructional materials for secondary schools.* Washington, DC: American Institute of Biological Sciences.

National Research Council (NRC). 1996. *National science education standards.* Washington, DC: National Academy Press.

Schmidt, W. H, McKnight, C., Cogan, L. S., Jakwerth, P. M., and Houang, R. T. 1999. *Facing the consequences—Using TIMSS for a closer look at U.S. mathematics and science.* The Netherlands: Kluwer Academic Publisher.

Shulman, L. S. 1986. Those who understand: Knowledge growth in teaching. *Educational Researcher* 15(2): 4–14.

Thompson, C. L., and Zeuli, J. S. 1999. The frame and the tapestry. In L. Darling-Hammond and G. Sykes, eds., *Teaching as the learning profession: Handbook of policy and practice.* San Francisco: Jossey-Bass.

Professional Development and How Teachers Learn: Developing Expert Science Teachers

Katherine E. Stiles and Susan Mundry

Katherine E. Stiles is a principal investigator/project director for several science education and professional development projects at WestEd, including the National Academy for Science and Mathematics Education Leadership. She has also worked with the Center for Science, Mathematics, and Engineering Education at the National Research Council and the National Institute for Science Education on projects focused on national science education standards and professional development. Prior to WestEd, she was a science curriculum developer at the National Science Resources Center for the Science and Technology for Children Project. Among her publications is the book *Designing Professional Development for Teachers of Science and Mathematics*, co-authored with close friend and colleague Susan Loucks-Horsley.

Susan Mundry is a project director at WestEd where she oversees several initiatives on leadership and professional development. Prior to this she was a senior research associate for the National Institute for Science Education, where she investigated different approaches to professional development for teachers in science and mathematics. She consults with organizations and school districts throughout the United States, providing learning experiences in the areas of leadership development, organizational change, and adult learning. She is the co-developer of the "Change Games," two simulation games on organizational change, called *Making Change for School Improvement* and *Systems Thinking/Systems Changing*. She is co-author of several books and articles, including *Leading Every Day: 124 Actions for Effective Leadership* and *Designing Successful Professional Meetings and Conferences in Education*.

By definition, experts have developed particular ways to think and reason effectively. Understanding expertise is important because it provides insights into the nature of thinking and problem solving. It is not simply general abilities, such as memory or intelligence, nor the use of general strategies that differentiate experts from novices. Instead, experts have acquired extensive knowledge that affects what they notice and how they organize, represent, and interpret information in their environments. This, in turn, affects their abilities to remember, reason, and solve problems. (Bransford, Brown, and Cocking 1999, 19).

In a Boston area school district, every teacher of science is assigned a mentor who has extensive expertise in science education and inquiry. One teacher and her mentor meet regularly before and after school and have time to observe one another's classrooms. Prior to observation, the teacher asks her mentor to observe certain key areas she has targeted for improvement and to later provide feedback in these areas. Her mentor reviews lesson plans, walks through the lesson with her, and asks key questions, such as: What do you predict the students will be thinking about? What problems do you anticipate they will have with the concepts you are teaching? What connections are there to the students' prior learning and how will you make those connections in the classroom? How will you assess your students and yourself as you are teaching? These questions help to model the kind of thinking one expects of an expert teacher, and over time the teacher begins to ask herself these questions.

After the teacher attends professional learning sessions, she meets with her mentor to think through how the new learning applies to the teaching of science, providing coherence among her many professional development experiences. As the teacher develops her expertise over time, she will also learn to mentor other new or novice teachers.

Groundbreaking research on learning and cognition has produced many new insights into how people learn. These findings conclusively dispel the idea that short-term and isolated learning experiences can produce powerful learning. This is especially true for teacher learning, given the complexity of teaching and the multifaceted role expert teachers must play. The research summarized in *How People Learn: Brain, Mind, Experience, and School* (Bransford, Brown, and Cocking 1999), along with research on effective professional development for teachers of science (see sidebar, "Principles of Effective Science Professional Development"), suggests that teacher learning programs must become more collegial and in-depth, longer in duration, and tailored to the experience levels of the learners, be they novice or expert teachers.

Professional development of teachers is clearly an essential element of science education reform. All of the major improvement initiatives call for increasing teacher knowledge and skills because of the link between student achievement and teacher knowledge and skill. Research shows that teacher expertise can account for about 40 percent of the variance on students' learning in reading and mathematics achievement—more than any other single factor, including student background (Ferguson 1991.) Other studies show a similar correlation between teacher expertise and student achievement across the subject areas.

Since teacher expertise has such a demonstrated impact on student learning, it stands to reason that programs that develop teachers' knowledge and skills are a sound investment in improving student outcomes. However, the research on learning (Bransford, Brown, and Cocking 1999) and that on effective teacher development (Sparks and Hirsch 1997; Loucks-Horsley, et al. 1998) suggests that teacher development as carried out in most schools today is not designed to develop the teacher expertise needed to bring about improved student learning. "The content of professional development is largely techniques, its pedagogy is training, and the learning it promotes consists of remembering new things to try in the classroom" (Thomson and Zeuli 1999, 353).

Principles of Effective Science Professional Development

To be effective, science professional development
- Must be driven by a vision of effective classroom learning and teaching that
  - is based on the belief that students, and their teachers, learn science best by *doing* science, by investigating for themselves, and by building their own understanding,
  - promotes inquiry-based learning, problem solving, student investigation and discovery, and application of knowledge,
  - encourages an in-depth understanding of core concepts in science, not just breadth of coverage, and
  - is committed to the concept that *all children* can and should learn science.
- Helps teachers gain knowledge and skills to broaden teaching by
  - deepening teachers' knowledge of the discipline of science, strengthening their knowledge of how children learn, and helping them make good decisions about curriculum materials.
- Mirrors methods to be used by students by
  - using instructional methods with teachers that they will use with students,
  - providing ample time for in-depth investigations, collaborative work, and reflection, and
  - connecting explicitly with teachers' other professional development experiences and activities.
- Builds a learning community by making continuous learning a part of the school norms and culture and encouraging teachers to take risks.
- Develops teacher leadership by encouraging teachers to serve in leadership roles such as supporters of other teachers, agents of change, and promoters of reform.
- Has links to the system, in that activities are aligned with curriculum frameworks, academic standards, and assessment as well as local policy, curriculum, and other teacher development initiatives.
- Is continuously assessed through on-going evaluation guides and reshapes the initiative as it proceeds.

Adapted from Loucks-Horsley, S., Stiles, K., and Hewson, P. 1996. Principles of effective professional development for mathematics and science education: A synthesis of standards. *NISE Brief* 1 (1). Madison, WI: National Institute for Science Education, University of Wisconsin-Madison.

The professional development systems and structures in most schools need to be redesigned to develop and support capable, knowledgeable, and expert teachers. Expert science teachers are those who

◆ *know the structure of the knowledge in their disciplines;*

◆ *know the conceptual barriers that are likely to hinder learning;*

◆ *have a well-organized knowledge of concepts (content knowledge) and inquiry procedures (based on pedagogical content knowledge); and*

◆ *continuously assess their own learning, knowledge, and practices.* (Bransford, Brown, and Cocking 1999, 230)

Novice teachers have not had the experience in the teaching role to develop in-depth knowledge in these areas. They need support and guidance to develop expertise in their disciplines, to recognize the conceptual barriers students typically encounter in science instruction and inquiry, and to employ strategies for assessing and adjusting their own learning practices. Sadly, few teachers have professional development focused in these areas. Rather, most are treated to "how to" workshops and activities that provide them with a "scrapbook" of learning rather than the coherent portfolio they need.

If school-based professional development programs are to gain a return on their professional development investment in terms of student learning, educators must transform their programs for professional learning, provide professional development that reflects how people learn, and build teacher expertise over time. Building teacher expertise should become the very purpose of all professional learning in schools.

Research on professional development calls for experiences that are designed to address the particular needs and developmental levels of adult learners. There are no models for one-size-fits-all (Loucks-Horsley, Stiles, and Hewson 1998). Teachers, like other learners, develop over time from novice to experienced to expert teacher. The learning opportunities they have will determine whether they reach the expert level. To facilitate this process, teachers need professional development tied to a career-long continuum of increasingly complex learning about their profession (Mundry, et al. 1999).

There are clear distinctions between novices and experts, and there are differences in the ways in which novice teachers and expert teachers learn in any professional development setting. For example, in the opening vignette a novice teacher is deepening her learning in the areas of science content and pedagogy and becoming comfortable as a new teacher. Her mentor is learning too, but her learning is very different. Even when experts and novices are in the same professional development situation, their learning is different because of how they process the experience. For example, in a recent gathering of teachers for professional learning, one of the authors showed a videotape of science learning. As the discussion unfolded it became clear that there was a wide range of expertise in the room. Novice teachers focused their comments more on the setup of the classroom and what the teacher did. The more experienced teachers reflected on what the students were doing and saying and what it meant for changes in the teacher's instruction. Expert teachers were wondering what the teacher was thinking and how she would assess herself. After the discussion, one teacher pointed out that while we all *watched* the same video, we all didn't *see* the same video.

According to research, experts have extensive knowledge that affects their perceptions and how they process information that they take in. This affects what they remember, how they reason, and how they solve problems. The research suggests that experts

◆ *notice features and meaningful patterns of information that are not noticed by novices;*

◆ *have a great deal of content knowledge that is organized, and their organization of information reflects a deep understanding of the subject matter; and*

◆ *are able to retrieve important aspects of their knowledge with little additional effort.* (Bransford, Brown, and Cocking 1999, xiii.)

Ideally, professional development programs would build such expertise in teachers. To do so they must be carefully designed with the goal of moving novice and experienced teachers to the expert level. One of the areas of research that sheds considerable light on the ways in which professional development for all teachers of science should be designed for this task is the transfer of learning. For teachers, this means that the knowledge and skills learned in professional development settings is transferred into teaching practices in the classroom. According to the authors of *How People Learn* (Bransford, Brown, and Cocking 1999), there are several key characteristics of learning and transfer that enhance the development of expert teachers:

◆ *initial learning is necessary for transfer, and a considerable amount is known about the kinds of learning experiences that support transfer;*

◆ *knowledge that is overly contextualized can reduce transfer;*

◆ *transfer is best viewed as an active, dynamic process rather than a passive end-product of a particular set of learning experiences; and*

◆ *all new learning involves transfer based on previous learning.* (41)

Although it seems clear that the extent to which initial learning is deeply understood will influence the extent to which that new learning will be extended into new areas, it is a critical aspect of transfer. The classic videotape from The Private Universe Project in Science (Harvard-Smithsonian Center for Astrophysics 1995) illustrates how critical a deep understanding of content and concepts is to solving problems and transferring initial learning to a new situation. On the videotape, several Harvard students are interviewed on the day of their graduation. They are given a wire, a light bulb, and a battery and asked to light the bulb. Each graduate initially claims he or she can easily light the bulb. However, after several trial and error attempts, only one graduate successfully lights the bulb and none of the other students can explain why their attempts might have been unsuccessful. The alarming aspect of this video is that highly educated graduates cannot complete a task that is essentially grounded in the concept of basic electric circuitry. What seems apparent is that these students did not learn the conceptual basis of electric circuitry and were therefore unable to create a complete circuit given new materials.

We can assume that these graduates passed numerous exams, engaged in laboratory exercises, and memorized volumes of content. However, we must conclude that they did not actually *learn* the concept of electric circuitry. Simply demonstrating rote knowledge does not imply deep understanding or learning. Without learning with understanding, transfer to new situations or contexts rarely occurs.

It is important to keep in mind that learning with understanding takes time. Teachers, like students, need time to process new learning, develop the ability to recognize patterns, receive feedback on their understanding, and connect the new learning to existing knowledge. Additionally, time to consider contexts for when and where the new learning can be applied is necessary for transfer. Explicit attention within the professional development context must be given to understanding how to translate the new knowledge into teaching practices. Additionally, it is the process of active, deliberate engagement that leads to learning with understanding and, ultimately, transfer. Again, this does not occur overnight. It takes time for initial learning to be assimilated into existing knowledge patterns and for teachers to begin to see how it connects to new situations and to their teaching practices. It requires that learners have the opportunity to explicitly focus on the implications of what they have learned and to monitor their own understanding. Recognizing that all new knowledge is filtered through the lens of prior knowledge can help learners be alert for misconceptions. The process of personal reflection and self-monitoring, as well as feedback from others, enhances the likelihood that learners will become aware of misconceptions and alter their previous understandings, rather than assimilate the new knowledge into misconceptions.

The ability to transfer learning into their classrooms is only one characteristic of expert teachers. As noted above, research and practice-based experience also inform us that "experts have acquired extensive knowledge that affects what they notice and how they organize, represent, and interpret information in their environment. This, in turn, affects their abilities to remember, reason, and solve problems" (Bransford, Brown, and Cocking 1999, 19). Experts organize knowledge around core concepts and essential patterns in their disciplines. For example, unlike the Harvard graduates, expert electrical engineers have a conceptual understanding of electric circuitry on which all of their knowledge is built. That understanding provides the groundwork on which they solve new problems and apply existing knowledge to new situations and it informs how they analyze unfamiliar challenges. They have not simply memorized the procedure for how to connect a circuit.

Similarly, the expert teacher does not implement every teaching strategy learned in a workshop. Rather, the expert teacher analyzes the appropriateness of any teaching strategy in light of what he or she knows about the subject matter content and the ways in which students will best learn that content. The expert teacher understands that students come to any subject with prior understandings—and often with misconceptions—and implements strategies designed specifically to help students analyze for themselves how the new knowledge fits with prior knowledge. The expert teacher also thinks on his or her feet, responding to new challenges in the classroom with a deep understanding of content and pedagogical content knowledge.

Professional development as viewed as the process through which teachers become expert teachers should provide opportunities for all teachers to develop the following characteristics of experts:

◆ Make connections and recognize meaningful patterns between new knowledge and guiding concepts or principles, rather than know a list of facts.

◆ Deeply understand the new knowledge and connect it to previous knowledge.

◆ Learn new content within multiple contexts and apply that new knowledge to unfamiliar contexts.

◆ Practice and implement new learning, with the goal of becoming "fluent at recognizing problem types in particular domains…so that appropriate solutions can be easily retrieved from memory" (Bransford, Brown, and Cocking 1999, 32).

◆ Develop the ability to reflect on and monitor understanding and recognize when misconceptions or misunderstandings occur, seeking new information with which to interpret and understand.

◆ Receive feedback from others and engage in collegial interactions.

Creating the conditions for teachers to engage in learning this way will require a more comprehensive approach to teacher learning, involving varied strategies as described below.

Designing Professional Development

…research evidence indicates that the most successful teacher professional development activities are those that are extended over time and encourage the development of teachers' learning communities. (Bransford, Brown, and Cocking 1999, 192)

If the ultimate goal of professional development is to develop expert teachers—teachers who are well-prepared with science content knowledge and pedagogical content knowledge—how far are we from this goal? The research on learning, transfer, and the development of experts suggests that professional development must necessarily include strategies for helping all teachers

◆ learn science content and the underlying foundational concepts in science;

◆ understand how students learn and think about science, including the misconceptions that students often have; and

◆ reflect on and analyze their own learning and understandings.

In the next section we discuss how each of these strategies can be used to help teachers become "expert."

Teachers' Development of Science Content and Concepts

Too often teachers are expected to attend a professional development workshop, learn new skills and knowledge, and immediately implement what they have learned in their classrooms. However, science content knowledge is rarely embedded within the professional development experience. For example, in the 1980s when new kit-based science programs were adopted by school districts across the country, teachers attended one-day orientation workshops to learn about the new programs and how to teach using hands-on materials. Frequently, those workshops consisted of opening the box of materials and walking through the procedural steps for how to manage the materials in the classroom. Rarely was in-depth attention given to the underlying concepts guiding the sequence of the lessons. Without an understanding of why specific activities were sequenced the way they were, teachers mechanically implemented the programs, often taking individual activities out of context and teaching them independently. Not only did students not learn the concepts being addressed through the activities, but teachers developed little understanding of those concepts themselves. The result was "hands-on, minds-off " science.

The development of science content knowledge is clearly articulated as a Teaching Standard in the *National Science Education Standards* (NRC 1996):

All teachers of science must have a strong, broad base of scientific knowledge extensive enough for them to:

◆ *Understand the nature of scientific inquiry, its central role in science, and how to use the skills and processes of scientific inquiry.*

◆ *Understand the fundamental facts and concepts in major science disciplines.*

◆ *Be able to make conceptual connections within and across science disciplines, as well as to mathematics, technology, and other school subjects.*

◆ *Use scientific understanding and ability when dealing with personal and societal issues. (NRC 1996, 59)*

As we are learning from current educational research, a focus on science content knowledge within professional development strategies is often still missing. In an annual study conducted by Horizon Research, Inc., of the National Science Foundation–funded reform projects in science and mathematics in school districts across the country, the most recent findings suggest that the majority of these projects fall short of realizing the goal of helping teachers deepen their science content knowledge.

Slightly fewer than 1 in 5 [professional development sessions for classroom teachers] included scientists or mathematicians as professional development providers, and only 2 in 5 had a major focus on increasing teacher content knowledge, raising the concern that the LSC [Local Systemic Reform] professional development does not emphasize adequately the need to deepen teacher disciplinary content knowledge. (Weiss, et al. 2001, 47)

However, there are notable approaches to professional development that are designed for the purpose of deepening teachers' science content knowledge. The Cohen and Hill (1998) study of mathematics reform in California found that when professional development workshops included direct and explicit attention to the disciplinary content intended to be taught through curriculum materials, teachers more often engaged in "best practice" teaching, with better student performance on state assessments. This type of situated learning of content that is grounded in the curriculum to be taught is a critical aspect of designing professional development experiences, specifically, curriculum implementation strategies.

It is important to keep in mind what the research says about "overly contextualized" learning. The authors of *How People Learn* synthesized the research on transfer of knowledge and concluded "knowledge that is overly contextualized can reduce transfer" (Bransford, Brown, and Cocking 1999, 41). While the Cohen and Hill (1998) study informs us that teachers best translate content knowledge into teaching practices when the content is taught within the realm of the curriculum, teachers also need the opportunity to transfer that new learning into varied teaching situations. One approach that can enhance understanding of when and where to use new knowledge is "contrasting cases." "Appropriately arranged contrasts can help people notice new features that previously escaped attention and learn which features are relevant or irrelevant to a particular concept" (Bransford, Brown, and Cocking 1999, 48). The opportunity to learn new knowledge within several contexts enhances the likelihood of transfer. In professional development settings, the use of science cases of science learning are an example of providing teachers with the opportunity to explore key features and characteristics of teacher and student learning in varied situations. (See example in sidebar, "WestEd's Science Case Methods Project.")

WestEd's Science Case Methods Project

Using teacher-written accounts of real-life classrooms to stimulate deep reflection and analysis, teachers meet with a WestEd facilitator for group discussion of classroom cases. The cases used in discussions are carefully crafted and field-tested to help teachers:

- acquire a deeper and more flexible knowledge of physical science content;
- hone their ability to see science concepts through the eyes of their students, creating the most effective instructional experience for student comprehension; and
- develop a mode of questioning which facilitates the teaching and learning of standards-based science.

When used in facilitated group discussion, cases prompt educators to frame problems in new ways, analyze situations and argue the benefits and drawbacks of various teaching methods.

For more information contact Mayumi Shinohara at WestEd (mayumi@wested.org).

In addition to curriculum implementation and case discussion strategies for science content knowledge development, teachers also can deepen their understanding of science content and concepts through immersion in the world of scientists. In this professional development strategy, teachers are immersed in an intensive experience in which they are able to pursue content in-depth, fully participate in the generation of investigable questions, conduct investigations that allow them to make meaning out of science inquiry activities, collect and analyze data, and gain a broader understanding of the science concepts they are investigating (Loucks-Horsley, et al. 1998).

Linked closely with this approach is explicit attention to transferring the new science content knowledge into the classroom. Teachers are expected not to simply learn the new content and translate it into a curriculum or learning activities. The most effective immersion in inquiry experiences also includes opportunities for teachers to experience the content and inquiry themselves and then reflect on it, first as a learner and then as a teacher. As teachers experience firsthand the process of sense-making and inquiring into the science phenomena they are investigating, they also need opportunities to reflect on how the nature of science learning influences their teaching practices. Teachers discover that since learning science is not just the transfer of information, but is focused on making sense of the content, they develop a deeper understanding of how they can guide students' learning rather than being the "sage on the stage." (See example in sidebar, "The Exploratorium Institute for Inquiry.")

Students' Learning and Thinking about Science

Understanding how students think about and learn science is critical to a teacher's ability to develop into an expert teacher. In his seminal articles, Lee Shulman defined pedagogical content knowledge as

The blending of content and pedagogy into an understanding of how particular topics, problems, or issues are organized, represented, and adapted to the diverse interests and abilities of learners, and presented for instruction. (1987, 8)

An understanding of what makes the learning of specific topics easy or difficult: the conceptions and preconceptions that students of different ages and backgrounds bring with them to the learning…. If those preconceptions are misconceptions, which they so often are, teachers need knowledge of the strategies most likely to be fruitful in reorganizing the understanding of learners. (1986, 9–10)

Integrating pedagogical content knowledge and science content knowledge into the profession of teaching is obviously critical. Unfortunately, help-

> ## The Exploratorium Institute for Inquiry
>
> At The Exploratorium Institute for Inquiry, in San Francisco, California, the professional development is deeply rooted in the belief that human beings are natural inquirers and that inquiry is at the heart of all learning. Educators personally experience the process of learning science through inquiry to stimulate thinking about how to create classrooms that are supportive environments for children's inquiry. Scientists and other educators guide teachers through the inquiry process. As teachers engage in investigations they develop a deeper understanding of science content and the inquiry process. They also work collaboratively with other teachers to explore the application of their new knowledge and skills in the classroom.
>
> For more information contact Lynn Rankin at The Exploratorium (lynnr@exploratorium.edu).

ing teachers develop this knowledge is often missing in teachers' learning opportunities. The Horizon Research, Inc., study of district-based mathematics and science reform projects across the country found that "only 30 percent of observed [professional development] sessions included helping teachers understand student thinking/ learning about mathematics or science content, an area that is increasingly being identified as important in teacher development" (Weiss, et al. 2001, 47). Without opportunities to understand how students think about and learn science concepts and principles, teachers' professional learning is incomplete.

Several professional development strategies are designed specifically to help teachers better understand the conceptions and misconceptions that students bring to science and the ways in which students process and learn new content. Examining student work—whether artifacts from the classroom or videotape of student discussions—involves analyzing student work and student thinking to enhance teachers' awareness of students' understanding of science concepts. Through facilitated and collaborative examination of student work, teachers focus on the reasoning and ex-

Continuous Assessment in Science Education

This professional development model supports teachers to conduct continuous assessment of science learning in the classroom. Through the model, teachers learn to continuously gather student work and analyze student thinking to inform their instruction. The professional development focuses on providing teachers with opportunities to:

- see the practices of inquiry and continuous assessment modeled;
- experience inquiry and continuous assessment as adult learners;
- practice inquiry and continuous assessment in classrooms with support from peers and center staff;
- increase conceptual understanding of science content; and
- reflect with peers and center staff on theory, personal strengths and challenges, and integrating inquiry and continuous assessment into existing practices.

For more information contact Maura Carlson at WestEd (maurac@wested.org).

planations students provide to describe specific phenomena or activities. One way teachers do this is to engage in continuous or formative classroom assessment that involves record keeping and observation in the classroom followed by analysis and reflection. (See example in sidebar, "Continuous Assessment in Science Education.") Often, examining student work is the content for study groups or the focus of a case discussion. Discussing and analyzing what the students write and say can provide critical insight into what students think and know. Coupled with a focus on developing teaching strategies to address students' understandings and misunderstandings, this professional development strategy can result in teachers who are critically aware of what students are learning in science. They use this knowledge to make instructional choices that deepen student understanding.

Teachers engaged in action research with a focus on student learning also have the opportunity to increase their understanding of student learning and thinking in science. In this approach, teachers ask a specific question and design a research study to obtain data. These data can include observation, anecdotal records, checklists, videotaping, collections of student work and writing, and interviewing. Once the data are collected, teachers analyze their data to enhance their understanding of the concepts that students do and do not understand. Teaching strategies that might more appropriately help students learn those concepts can then be explored and implemented. "Teacher research helps link classroom practices with results. If teachers discover that certain strategies are more effective than others for presenting science content, they are more likely to make greater use of them and abandon use of less effective ones" (Loucks-Horsley, et al. 1998, 97). Action research is also a strategy that enhances the professional learning culture in schools. When teachers collaborate on investigating their teaching practices and their students' learning, "teachers' beliefs about learning, their students, and their conceptions of themselves as learners are explicitly examined, challenged, and supported" (Bransford, Brown, and Cocking 1999, 187).

Teachers' Reflection on Their Learning and Understandings

A great deal has been written about the effects on teachers and their teaching as a result of reflecting on their work through collaborative discussions in learning communities. As Darling-Hammond and McLaughlin (1999) note, "As recent research has argued, the possibilities for individual teacher learning increase greatly as professional communities move from individualistic or 'balkanized' cultures to 'collaborative' cultures, and towards what can be described as 'learning communities'" (380). One critical aspect of these learning communities is a focus on lifelong learning through the process of continued reflection and seeking opportunities to learn. "Genuine teacher learning communities—those with a demonstrable effect on teaching and learning—are those that question and challenge teaching routines when they prove ineffective with students and that routinely examine new conceptions of subject and teaching" (Little 1999, 255).

Unfortunately, too many schools continue to organize themselves around isolated classrooms with little or no time for teacher interaction or collaboration. Teaching is conducted behind closed doors and teachers have few opportunities to plan lessons together or explore teaching and learning issues. Similarly, professional learning is often viewed as the formal after-school workshop and not as practice-embedded learning. What is most critically lacking in schools is a culture that values time for teachers to interact professionally and reflect on their practice and student learning.

Self-monitoring and reflection on thinking, learning, and practice are essential for professional expertise and learning is enhanced when these practices are conducted with colleagues (Bransford, Brown, and Cocking 1999). However, collegial arrangements for professional development alone are not enough to produce expert teachers. They must be coupled with a focus on developing content and pedagogical content knowledge (Thompson and Zeuli 1999.) Several professional development strategies provide structures for formal and ongoing reflection and processing. The strategies noted earlier—curriculum implementation, immersion in the world of scientists, case discussions, study groups, examining student work, and action research—are all strategies that have the greatest impact on teacher learning when conducted collegially.

In addition, coaching and mentoring (as described in the opening vignette) provide structures within which teachers can partner with each other to improve teaching and learning through observation, feedback, problem solving, and co-designing. Novice teachers often are focused on managing the learning environment and not as consciously aware of their interactions with students or their own thinking about their teaching. Expert teachers, on the other hand, are frequently conscious of their students' thinking and understanding as well as the strategies they as teachers implement to guide students' learning. Partnering the novice and expert teacher to examine practice can enhance the novice teacher's awareness of his or her teaching practices and the learning of the students. Similarly, coaches and mentors provide valuable support and guidance to novice teachers.

Conclusions and Recommendations

The focus of professional development should shift from implementation of the latest techniques to a coherent program of developing expert teachers. Such learning opportunities for all teachers would have these features:

◆ Engagement with activities explicitly designed to developing science content knowledge, with a deep understanding of the underlying principles of science

◆ Opportunities to help teachers understand how students think about and learn science, including the misconceptions students often have and how to challenge them

◆ New learning that is based on prior knowledge and learning

◆ Opportunities for learning within varied contexts

◆ Time for collaboration and interactions with colleagues within the structure of the school day

◆ Time and structures for reflection and analysis of learning and understandings

◆ Opportunities to help teachers recognize patterns and connections (e.g., across the curriculum)

◆ Continued learning experience over time and with depth

◆ Ample opportunities for translating new learning into teaching strategies

To reach this vision of professional development, we conclude that schools and school districts must rethink and redesign professional learning opportunities for teachers. We recommend that

◆ all teachers develop and continually update a tailored professional learning plan tied to an assessment of their own knowledge and skills and play an active role in selecting their professional development experiences;

◆ all teachers document and reflect on their professional development experiences to identify further needs and make connections across their various experiences;

◆ all teachers have access to quality, in-depth instruction in science content and curriculum and opportunities to interact with colleagues about teaching and learning issues;

◆ all school districts provide coordination, funding, and administrative support for teachers to have in-depth, collegial, and ongoing profession learning experiences matched to their individual professional learning plans; and

◆ school districts enter into partnerships with professional associations, businesses, local universities and/or other organizations that have demonstrated capacity to provide quality science content learning and to deepen knowledge of teaching and learning.

References

Bransford, J. D., Brown, A. L., and Cocking, R. R., eds. 1999. *How people learn: Brain, mind, experience, and school.* Washington, DC: National Academy Press.

Cohen, D. K., and Hill, H. C. 1998. State policy and classroom performance: Mathematics reform in California. *CPRE Policy Briefs* (RB-23-May). Philadelphia: Consortium for Policy Research in Education (CPRE), Graduate School of Education, University of Pennsylvania.

Darling-Hammond, L., and McLaughlin, M. W. 1999. Investing in teaching as a learning profession: Policy problems and prospects. In L. Darling-Hammond and G. Sykes, eds., *Teaching as the learning profession: Handbook of policy and practice,* 376-411. San Francisco: Jossey-Bass.

Ferguson, R. F. 1991. Paying for public education: New evidence on how and why money matters. *Harvard Journal on Legislation* 28 (2): 465-98.

Little, J. W. 1999. Organizing schools for teacher learning. In L. Darling-Hammond and G. Sykes, eds., *Teaching as the learning profession: Handbook of policy and practice,* 233-62. San Francisco: Jossey-Bass.

Loucks-Horsley, S., Hewson, P. W., Love, N., and Stiles, K. E. 1998. *Designing professional development for teachers of science and mathematics.* Thousand Oaks, CA: Corwin Press.

Loucks-Horsley, S., Stiles, K., and Hewson, P. 1996. Principles of effective professional development for mathematics and science education: A synthesis of standards. *NISE Brief* 1 (1). Madison, WI: National Institute for Science Education, University of Wisconsin.

Mundry, S., Spector, B., Loucks-Horsley, S. and Morrison, N. 1999. From novice to pro: Improving science and mathematics teaching by improving teacher learning. *Education Week* 19 (14): 21.

National Research Council (NRC). 1996. *National science education standards.* Washington, DC: National Academy Press.

Shulman, L. S. 1986. Those who understand: Knowledge growth in teaching. *Educational Researcher* 15 (2): 4-14.

————. 1987. Knowledge and teaching: foundations of the new reform. *Harvard Educational Review* 57 (1): 1-22.

Sparks, D., and Hirsh, S. 1997. *A new vision for staff development.* Alexandria, VA: Association for Supervision and Curriculum Development and Oxford, OH: National Staff Development Council.

Thompson, C. L., and Zeuli, J. S. 1999. The frame and the tapestry: Standards-based reform and professional development. In L. Darling-Hammond and G. Sykes, eds., *Teaching as the learning profession: Handbook of policy and practice,* 341-75. San Francisco: Jossey-Bass.

Weiss, I. R., Arnold, E. E., Banilower, E. R., and Soar, E. H. 2001. *Local systemic change through teacher enhancement: Year six cross-site report.* Chapel Hill, NC: Horizon Research.